Lord Longford's Prison Diary

W0226796

For Elizabeth

LORD LONGFORD'S
Prison Diary

LORD LONGFORD

Edited by Peter Stanford

A LION BOOK

Copyright © 2000 Lord Longford
Editor's Preface and Interview with Lord Longford
copyright © 2000 Peter Stanford

The author asserts the moral right
to be identified as the author of this work

Published by
Lion Publishing plc
Sandy Lane West, Oxford, England
www.lion-publishing.co.uk
ISBN 0 7459 5001 9

First edition 2000
10 9 8 7 6 5 4 3 2 1 0

All rights reserved

A catalogue record for this book is available
from the British Library

Typeset in 10.75/14 Baskerville
Printed and bound in Great Britain by
Biddles Ltd, Guildford and King's Lynn

Contents

Editor's Preface

Frank Longford has been a prison visitor for over sixty years. In his ninety-fifth year and almost blind, this former Labour Cabinet minister still visits several prisoners a week, travelling to all corners of the country by public transport to see people who often have no one else to turn to for support. It is a remarkable one-man mission, much lampooned and much misunderstood in the press on account of his alleged penchant for sitting down opposite notorious murderers and disgraced politicians.

While most of us recoil from the prospect of looking sex offenders or killers or drug traffickers in the eye, preferring to press politicians to keep such people behind bars, and therefore separated from us for as long as possible, Frank Longford tries to stretch out the hand of friendship, of understanding and of common humanity. However appealing the 'lock-them-up-and-throw-away-the-key' school of thought, it is impractical in the final analysis. The vast majority of prisoners, however appalling their crimes, will one day be released. Frank Longford is being resolutely pragmatic by attempting to understand them during their sentence and trying to ensure that their treatment in prisons is as enlightened and potentially reforming as possible, so that they may one day re-enter society as full and contributing members.

This diary is his own contemporaneous account of four years of travelling, stretching from the autumn of 1995 to the summer of 1999. It should help explain some of his more public – and publicized – gestures towards prisoners. In detailing his visits to Myra Hindley, for instance, it touches on the reasons behind his long-running campaign to free the Moors murderess and their often turbulent relationship.

It also includes accounts of encounters with other well-known criminals – Hindley's accomplice, Ian Brady; mass murderer, Denis Nilsen; drug dealer, Eddie Richardson; spy, Michael Bettaney; and disgraced former Cabinet minister, Jonathan Aitken. But these 'big names' make up only a small section of the cast. Contrary to popular legend, the majority of Frank Longford's friends behind bars are known only to their victims and to those who guard them under lock and key. Never condoning what they have done, he nonetheless feels that they should not be denied human contact. As a committed Christian, he follows to the letter a very simple and direct gospel imperative: 'I was in prison and you came to see me.'

In an age ever more obsessed with crime and ever more hard-hearted about the punishment of criminals, his can be a lonely and misunderstood witness. Yet, in spite of advancing years, unkind attacks in the press, sneers from younger ministers who forget that he was once a first-division politician tipped by Clement Attlee as a future prime minister, and even the open hostility of prison officials, Frank Longford trudges on regardless.

His position as a former Cabinet minister and his long-time parliamentary platform in the House of Lords makes him a surprisingly effective spokesman for prisoners' grievances with the Home Office and prison authorities. The diary contains numerous examples of when a letter from him to a governor or a minister has brought about positive change in everyday conditions for an individual prisoner. These small things may seem as nothing compared with the powers that a Cabinet minister wields, but for him they are at the very heart of what he is trying to do.

There is a third group of prisoners included in the

diary, namely men and women whom Frank Longford believes are either innocent of the crimes of which they are accused – like the pregnant Roisin McAliskey, facing extradition on terrorism charges to a country she says she has never even visited – or are unsuited to serve their sentence in prison because of their mental problems. He is a tireless campaigner on their behalf.

Moreover he remains one of the few public figures with a continuing belief in the power of prison not only to reform, but also, in his own terms, to redeem individuals. In an age of ever more draconian attitudes to criminals, Frank Longford's remains an isolated voice but, set in the context of this diary and his first-hand experiences, it should not be lightly dismissed.

Threaded through the text is his correspondence with ministers, both in the Conservative administration and later under Labour, his vendetta against Michael Howard, his attempts to influence Tony Blair and Jack Straw on prisons' policy, and his broader reflections on the need for prison reform, a subject which has concerned him both as a minister and now as a campaigner. There are also moments of humour and self-deprecation.

He offers three unique perspectives in this diary, first on prisons' policy over sixty years, second on what actually goes on in the name of justice in Britain's jails, and third on what goes on inside prisoners' heads and hearts. Frank Longford, more than any other outsider, has had the opportunity to understand the criminal psyche.

The diary touches fleetingly on his own past career and his continuing reputation in the gossip columns as a champagne socialist and party-goer, surrounded either by his wife, Elizabeth, the royal biographer, his glamorous and talented daughters, the writers, Rachel Billington, Judith Kazantzis and Antonia Fraser, or his son-in-law, Harold

Pinter. The distance from 10 Downing Street receptions to Wormwood Scrubs would seem to many unbridgeable, but Frank Longford makes his own attempt, often flawed but always sincere, to find a role in both worlds.

I have come to the task of editing this diary fresh from writing an admiring but critical biography of Frank Longford, published in 1994. As part of the process of researching the biography I ended up following in his footsteps and visiting prisons and prisoners, including Myra Hindley. It left me with two enduring impressions. The first was a determination to do something, to follow in some necessarily minor way in Frank Longford's footsteps in fighting to change society's currently appalling attitude to prisoners. I hope editing this remarkable and enlightening diary will be a first small step in that direction.

The second was a profound admiration for all that Frank Longford has sought to achieve. As a politician he aimed high and failed. The second son of a Protestant Anglo-Irish ascendancy family, born in 1905, he is a double convert to Catholicism and socialism. After trying his hand at journalism, and later teaching at Oxford, he shone briefly in Clement Attlee's post-war government, leaving his mark as the British minister responsible for starting the reconstruction of occupied Germany. Conrad Adenauer counted him among the founders of West Germany, but at home he was condemned for being soft on Britain's erstwhile enemies.

Later he wanted to be a reforming Home Secretary, but the death of his great friend and patron Hugh Gaitskell, in 1963, pushed him to the margins of the Labour party. Frank Longford spent his time in Harold Wilson's Cabinet of the mid-1960s as Leader of the House of Lords, Lord Privy Seal and, briefly, Colonial Secretary, none of them posts that put him in the mainstream. He was, by his own admission, ineffective and his resignation in 1968 over the government's failure to honour an election pledge to raise the school-leaving age to sixteen was regarded as inevitable and little mourned. *Punch* marked the event with a poem:

Lord Longford steeled his mighty mind
Gritted his molars, and resigned.
How sad for his heroic pose
The headlines 'Only Longford Goes'.

Yet in the field of prison reform he has done much of which he can be proud. In 1955 he set up the first organisation in this country dedicated to the welfare of ex-prisoners. The New Bridge, with which he is still involved, was the forerunner of many of today's care and rehabilitation organisations. By initiating a series of debates in the Lords based around the learned reports on prisons' policy he produced in the 1950s and 1960s, Frank Longford awakened the conscience of the Palace of Westminster to the question of prison reform. Today there is a well-organised all-party lobbying group which carries on that work. And in 1964 he chaired the committee of inquiry that later persuaded Harold Wilson to introduce the probation system which remains with us to this day.

In one sense, Frank Longford belongs more in the nineteenth century than the twentieth and twenty-first. He stands in the philanthropic tradition of Lords Wilberforce and Shaftesbury. Like them born into privilege, like them a devout Christian determined to translate faith into action, Frank Longford has attempted, as they did, to use his political savvy to win over a hostile Establishment to the cause of far-reaching social reform. All three men fall into the category of archetypal do-gooders, combining a principled, almost naïve clear-sightedness with shrewdness, in playing their political cards to achieve their ends. Wilberforce tackled the slave trade, Shaftesbury conditions in the factories and mines, and Frank Longford the penal system. Where his forerunners succeeded, he has only aspired. For all his other achievements, there is no single piece of legislation that bears his name. Six decades after he made his first visit to Oxford Jail, the conditions and prejudices he meets in Britain's prisons still horrify him.

What is left that is unique, however, is his personal crusade, his apostolate to prisoners. It may not affect the course of public policy greatly or change laws, but it does change lives – the lives of those he visits and of those like me and many others who observe him. It should not therefore be underestimated. It should certainly not be laughed off as a foolish old man's odd taste for intimacy with supposedly wicked men and women. Rather it should be a subject of celebration, and more importantly respect. My hope is that this diary may contribute, belatedly, to that process.

The diary entries themselves prompt many questions about Frank Longford's more general attitude to crime and punishment. I have therefore collected together a list of queries that occurred to me, added to them from the many articles and individuals who publicly doubt the wisdom of his crusade, and sought his answers in a section that follows the diary. I hope his responses give a wider context to his day-to-day remarks.

To the same end, I have also included a brief selection of his writings on prisons' policy over the period covered by the diary.

There were moments in going through these diaries when contemporary political correctness or my own deep-seated beliefs, which are not always, despite our shared Catholicism, in line with Frank Longford's on questions of personal morality, made me itch to delete or rewrite phrases and sections. But that would have been to attempt to show Frank Longford as a plaster saint. He is aware of his flaws and relishes others disagreeing with him. So it is his voice, unfiltered and at times strikingly out of step with the times, that sets the tone of this diary. Whatever mistakes he has made, he once told me, he will account for when he meets St Peter at the gates of heaven. He is, he added, expecting to spend some time in purgatory.

PETER STANFORD

Lord Longford's Prison Diary

Thursday October 19, 1995

Visited Roy in the prison hospital at Pentonville yesterday. I have known Roy for at least fifteen years in a variety of prisons. He has also been more than once in a mental home.

About a year ago he was charged with stealing £89,000 from the DSS. Not for the first time he took an overdose and was packed off unconscious to the Royal Free Hospital in Hampstead. Thence he escaped and was on the run in Morocco and Amsterdam for eight months.

On returning to England, in theory to give himself up, he was arrested, but took the habitual overdose and was back in the Royal Free. Taken to court eventually, he took yet another overdose and this time he is at Pentonville Prison. He tells me that he has not eaten for six weeks – longer than Christ's fast in the wilderness – and intends to starve himself to death. I am imploring his doctors (1) to prevent this happening, and (2) to land him in hospital rather than prison when he goes to court.

The chief medical officer at Pentonville is extremely sympathetic and favours both propositions. The psychiatrist at the Royal Free is having difficulty in reconciling the hospital solution with the existing law. In layman's language Roy is not 'bonkers' enough.

I can sympathise with all concerned. Roy expects to go to court next Friday. I have promised to be present, and, not for the first time, to give evidence to character if he is convicted. If I am asked the question in the witness box – 'Do you consider your friend a mental case?' – what the hell do I say?

Friday October 20, 1995

Lunch yesterday with Stephen Tumin, Chief Inspector of Prisons. He retires in a fortnight after eight years' service. He is much admired by all those whose opinions I value, but a strong critic of 'Howardism' – the penal policies of Home Secretary, Michael Howard. The essence of 'Howardism' is twofold. One, 'prison works'; two, it will work much better if made more unpleasant for prisoners. 'Howardism' has achieved the antagonism of all those most concerned with prisoners, the prison staffs from governor level downwards, and the Probation Service. The prison governors have taken the unprecedented step of issuing a manifesto sharply critical of their employers. Typical of the prison staff is an experienced officer who said to me recently, on one of my weekly visits to prisons, 'We know that Mr Howard would be unhappy if he saw a smile on a prisoner's face.'

Throughout his eight years Stephen has consistently demanded that prisons should be places of training, which fits in with the heavy emphasis on rehabilitation in the recent governors' manifesto. I cannot help remembering that, when I opened the first debate on prisons in the House of Lords in 1955, I urged that prison officers should become social workers. Today, Stephen, like David Evans, General Secretary of the Prison Officers' Association, is making the same demand. It is not likely to be achieved in my lifetime, but we must never lose sight of the ideal.

Saturday October 21, 1995

Yesterday morning visited Brian Vale at Wormwood Scrubs. He had answered a letter in a paper asking for a 'blind date'. The resulting relationship saw him fall in love with the woman but, when she rejected him in traumatic fashion, he killed her. He was found guilty of manslaughter with diminished responsibility and, rather unusually, given a life sentence. The judge apparently spoke very harshly of his character in court.

He was somewhat relieved to hear that the Appeal Court

took a different view of him and cut his tariff from ten years to eight. He still feels, as I do, that the life sentence was very unfair to him considering that he was not convicted of murder.

He is very intelligent and voluble and is capable, I believe, of doing well in his Open University work. He is a strong Labour supporter.

Wednesday October 25, 1995

Visited Roy. He was very cheerful when he learnt that the chief medical officer at Pentonville and the psychiatrist at the Royal Free Hospital in Hampstead were both going to recommend that he should be sectioned, that is, sent to hospital rather than prison.

Friday October 27, 1995

I made my way to a very remote court, the Crown Court at Snaresbrook in east London, where Roy's counsel argued eloquently that the judge should follow medical advice and section Roy. The judge, however, was very sticky. He wanted to know – perhaps not unreasonably – whether there was any assurance that the medical authorities would not let Roy out of hospital in a short time. As the charge against him is that he has fraudulently obtained £89,000 from the DSS the judge was, presumably, concerned about the public outcry if he obtained early discharge.

The case was adjourned for a fortnight.

Saturday October 28, 1995

Roy rang me up from Pentonville terribly depressed. Later I rang the prison and urged them to take special care of him.

Monday October 30, 1995

9.30 a.m. Rang Pentonville to ask whether Roy would like me to visit him as in previous weeks. I was told that he did not wish to see me. The acting medical officer, however, suggested that I should ring back at 12.30 to find out if that was confirmed. At 12.30 I rang back and was given the same answer.

2.30 p.m. Received a message that Roy would, after all, like to see me. So, made my way by tube from Westminster.

At Pentonville there is now a ridiculous new formality imposed in the interests of security. One is supposed to go to a visitors' centre before trying to enter the prison. On the last occasion I wasted half an hour there. Mercifully I am now excused this nonsense.

No one can say that Roy is not a man of conscience. He was genuinely worried at the thought of the pain his refusal to see me had caused. We had quite a happy visit. (Later in the week he rang in a state of elation – I hope justified. The chief medical officer appears to have assured him that he will get him into hospital instead of prison.)

Tuesday October 31, 1995

Entertained at lunch in the Lords by the secretary and assistant secretary of the Prison Governors' Association. I had recently met the assistant secretary at Cookham Wood Prison in Kent where she was then governor. I had been there visiting Myra Hindley before her transfer to Durham, and the governor joined us for half an hour's friendly chat.

Seeing these two impressive middle-aged ladies together, one would not have known which was governor and which was inmate. But the governor's friendliness towards Myra would appear to have been her undoing. The tabloid press insisted that Myra was leading a privileged life. The governor herself considered that John Kay, the chief reporter of *The Sun*, was the architect of her removal from office.

I had to confess to her that John Kay and I were friends, in spite of my intense disapproval of much of what he writes. He always insists that the references to Myra, as for example 'an evil monster', are not his but are imposed on his articles.

On the last occasion I told him that I had to withdraw from a lunch he had promised to give in honour of my ninetieth birthday. But I gave way when he told me that his wife would be much upset. The former governor took this with a good grace.

Thursday November 2, 1995

10 a.m. Visited Mark Tomlinson and Dean McGillicuddy in Downview Prison at Sutton in Surrey. Downview I find much sought after by prisoners in the later stages of their sentence. Mark and Dean were both making full use of their time, but in different ways.

Mark did not find the educational classes very helpful, but was working hard in his cell in the hopes of becoming a full-time counsellor when released. He was waiting for an answer from the Parole Board about his release on parole, but was just as happy at the possibility that he might go to Latchmere House at nearby Richmond.

I can well understand why the prisoners yearn to go to Latchmere House, where they work outside the prison as soon as it can be arranged.

Dean was as buoyant as ever. He comes from a tragic family. His brother, whom I have also visited several times, left home in his teens, became a drug addict, and has been in and out of prison ever since. His mother, a charming woman whom I have welcomed at the House of Lords, has spent much of her time in hospital.

Dean was going ahead in business when, in his own words, he became greedy. He was arrested and convicted of dealing in drugs. He admits that he was guilty.

But I agree with him in thinking fourteen years is a monstrous sentence. When Dean was convicted his father committed suicide. Dean will, I believe, make good in the end. He is working hard to become a clerk of works. I don't know anyone who is so determined to make the best use of his time in prison.

Back to the House of Lords and then to tea at Claridges with Niven Craig whom I had not seen for a number of years. We greeted one another as old friends. Niven is the elder brother of Christopher Craig who was convicted more than forty years ago of shooting a policeman in the course of a robbery. Because he was then just under sixteen he was not executed, but his accomplice, Derek Bentley, was hanged. Bentley's sister has campaigned ever since for a pardon which has been partly secured.

Niven and Christopher were the sons of a respected bank manager. Niven went wrong early, being packed off, as he reminded me, to an approved school in his teens. Later he spent twelve years in prison. With some hesitation I reminded him that soon after I joined the Wilson Cabinet, a Conservative MP reported me to the Prime Minister as having a homosexual relationship with Niven. I had become friendly with Christopher while he was in prison, and soon after the Niven allegation I was asked to Christopher's wedding.

Harold Wilson pressed me not to go and, rightly or wrongly, I agreed not to. I salved a bit of my conscience by giving Christopher and his bride-to-be a dinner the night before the wedding.

I told Niven that I had always felt guilty about all this. He said that he and Christopher had always understood.

I was glad to find that Niven was not only able to offer me

tea in Claridge's with his delightful and tall, good-looking son, but seemed thoroughly at home there. He is now sixty-nine and appears to have been, on the whole, successful in business. His charm was more evident than ever.

His son, aged twenty-seven, has now just completed a three-year drama course. Did I know of a good literary agent? I have since learnt from my daughter Antonia that Curtis Brown, the ever-helpful friend of so many of the family, has a theatrical section. I shall be approaching them forthwith.

Sunday November 19, 1995

I return to the diary after a fortnight. I have not been altogether idle in the meanwhile. Apart from the usual activities, I have written reviews for *The Catholic Herald* and *The Tablet*, and an article for *The Spectator* which should appear next Friday.

I refrained from mentioning penal reform in my article in *The Spectator*, which is entitled 'New Labour – Old or Both'. I insisted, however, that Tony Blair, a Christian socialist, must be expected to live up to the instruction in St Luke's Gospel: 'when thou makest a feast thou shalt call the poor, the maimed, the lame and the blind and thou shall be blessed.' I did not labour the point that prisoners and ex-prisoners must be treated with like generosity.

I have kept up my average of a prison a week by visiting three prisons in the week just concluded. A good deal of my energy has been expended on Roy. On Friday last week I made my way by tube and ultimately taxi to Snaresbrook Crown Court. It took me an hour and a quarter to get there and an hour and a quarter to get back. In between I waited an hour and three quarters for his case to come up, but had to leave without hearing it. I am glad that Roy was made aware of my presence and told correctly that I was spending the time on my Bible.

In the event Roy was to be sentenced a fortnight later and in the meanwhile to go to his old haunt the Royal Free Hospital at Hampstead (from which he escaped and went on the run for eight months). He was still in Pentonville Prison when I visited him last Tuesday (but was moved to the Royal Free the following day). He was very cheerful on Tuesday. I am hopeful that he will in fact be allowed to stay in the Royal Free until the doctors decide that he can safely be released.

On Monday, I visited Winston Silcot again in Maidstone Prison. Though he was eventually acquitted of the horrifying murder of P.C. Keith Blakelock during the Broadwater Farm riots, he was on bail at the time of the alleged murder and was subsequently found guilty of an earlier murder for which he is now serving life. On his own account he was approached by three enemies, all with knives. He hastily borrowed a knife from a friend and stabbed one of the assailants, killing him. His plea of self-defence did not succeed either at his trial or at the appeal.

He has now, however, obtained three more witnesses and, having spoken to his solicitor, it seems to me possible that he might procure another acquittal. A reference back to the Appeal Court, however, requires the permission of the Home Secretary. There seems to have been an unconscionable delay at the Home Office. I have agreed to write to Ann Widdecombe, Minister for Prisons, if the solicitor will assist me with the draft.

On Friday (November 17) I was taken by my old friend, the lawyer Andrew McCooey, and John Jennings, chairman of the local magistrates' bench and former chairman of the Board of Visitors at Swaleside Prison on the Isle of Sheppey, to meet a group of lifers in that prison. Andrew, in his mid-forties, conducts a one-man business in Sittingbourne, Kent, and from that base ranges far and wide across the world. He fought heroically, with my grandson by marriage, Edward

Fitzgerald, to save Sue Hagan and Sally Croft from being extradited to the United States in a well-publicised case over their role in a cult. I spoke on their behalf three times in the House of Lords. He and Edward have also laboured indomitably on behalf of Myra Hindley, though Andrew has recently had to hand over his role to another solicitor.

John Jennings and his wife entertained us handsomely at lunch. He, in his own way, is as dedicated as Andrew to the cause of prisoners.

About a dozen lifers came to the group. All but one who spoke had been convicted of murder. I have no means of knowing whether they were typical of the lifers generally. Inevitably they were more interested in their own individual cases than in the issues of principle I sought to raise: (1) who should be sentenced to life?; (2) what arrangements should be made for their release?; (3) and for their recall; and (4) how should they be treated in prison?

A very attractive young man of twenty-nine, who had been in prison eight years, had stabbed someone to death in the course of a robbery. The trial judge had recommended a tariff of seven years. It has been increased to twelve by the Lord Chief Justice, and the Home Secretary has increased it to fourteen.

Several others present had had their tariffs increased by the Home Secretary in the same way. The tariff is supposed to reflect the gravity of the crime. The Home Secretary retains the power to hold a prisoner in custody beyond the tariff date if he or she is thought to be dangerous. But the issue has recently become a very live one since Michael Howard was deemed by a High Court judge to have acted unlawfully in increasing a tariff set by the judiciary.

Up till now it has always been assumed that the release of a life prisoner depended entirely on the personal decision of the Home Secretary. Now it seems the judiciary is asserting a role which, in public discussion, was never allotted to them.

It is an ironical reflection that a few years ago penal reformers like myself looked upon the judges as a more reactionary force in sentencing than the politicians. We demanded, and perhaps still demand, a sentencing council to exercise some control over them. I have said many times, in this country we send more people per head of population to prison than any other country, and it is the judges who send them there.

But in the age of Howard and 'Howardism' we are looking upon the judges as relatively beneficent.

My own point of view about the release of life prisoners (leaving over the question of recall) can be summed up in this way: (1) one murder should not produce a mandatory life sentence; (2) where life sentences are proposed there should be a judicial review after a number of years, repeated where necessary at intervals. The prisoner should be allowed to appear and be represented before such a tribunal. I don't think that the last word can be said by the judge at the time of the trial when little is known about the prisoner and public feeling may be running high (e.g. the Moors murders). But nor should it be left to the unfettered discretion of the Home Secretary, guided all too often by political considerations. The parole system should be part of the machinery but, in the last resort, there must be a reference back to the courts.

Wednesday November 22, 1995

I addressed a religious gathering of undergraduates in Magdalen College, Oxford, on 'Christianity and Punishment'. As usual I was asked about Myra Hindley. What sort of woman was she? I caused some surprise by saying that she was probably as good a person as anyone in the room, except – I added as an afterthought – the priest sitting next to me. A heated argument followed. I argued that the saints had often insisted, as had Thomas à Kempis, that we must treat no one as worse than ourselves.

Thursday November 23, 1995

Visited Roy in the Royal Free Hospital. He was suffering from mild flu, but seemed confident that when he goes to court again on November 30 the judge will be compelled by the medical evidence to send him to hospital, not prison.

I have agreed to write a letter to the judge. I am by no means clear as to what form it should take. I could easily describe Roy as a man of genuine ability whom I have known for fifteen years and of whom I am very fond, but I am supposed to argue that he is 'bonkers'. This may take a little doing – though, in one sense, I agree with him and the doctors that he is.

Friday November 24, 1995

Yesterday I found myself at short notice taking part in the Radio 4 *Moral Maze* programme. The subject was with special reference to the case of Frederick and Rosemary West. He committed suicide some time ago, but she has just been convicted of ten murders.

As I sat and listened outside to the three previous speakers being interrogated, I found myself very critical (we all were) of the interviewing technique of the panel. It was like a viva being conducted by four *soi-disant* dons interrupting each other and the interviewees incessantly. When my turn came I was determined to make my two heartfelt points: (1) we must hate the sin and love the sinner; and (2) Jesus Christ came to seek and to save those who were lost.

One of the panel, an academic of some kind, began quoting the gospel against me. I asked him snappily, 'Are you a Christian?' and when he said he wasn't, derided him unkindly.

I was surprised to be told that, though this programme comes under the auspices of the religious affairs department, God is not usually mentioned.

Looking back I suppose I was ruder than I would have been under less heated conditions, and therefore should not be too proud of myself. I am bound to say, however, that I have since had a good many congratulations about my performance. For example, from the minister in charge of a Methodist service where I went on after leaving the *Moral Maze*.

Saturday November 25, 1995

Visited Whitemoor Prison in Cambridgeshire again yesterday. The new security measures applied to visitors are pretty ludicrous. If, for example, you want to buy a prisoner a cup of tea, you have to go over to a visiting centre a hundred yards or so from the prison, leave all money behind (bank notes as well as coins) and buy a ticket.

On entering the prison I was submitted to a nominal search four times before meeting a prisoner. On the last occasion the prison officer was equipped with a dog who sniffed me for drugs. I was a little too outspoken perhaps in my criticisms of the steps being taken. I always say I do exactly what I am told in prison and complain afterwards. But it is difficult not to seem to be criticising the officers searching one. Later on that day I said to a senior officer, 'These new restrictions are pretty tiresome for visitors.' He replied, 'They're much worse for us,' referring, I've no doubt, to relationships with the prisoners.

This time I visited, as often before, Eddie Richardson and Denis 'Des' Nilsen and Brett Mills, whom I last saw at High Point in Suffolk. Eddie, who is serving twenty-five years for importation of drugs, has discovered a true talent as a painter which has given a new meaning to his life. He is awaiting a decision as to whether he can come off 'category A'. The crucial point is that while he remains on it he cannot get parole.

He does not wish me to take up his case again until a decision is reached in the immediate future. I pressed the matter on Derek Lewis in a personal interview before the latter's removal as head of the Prison Service. The Home Office has, therefore, my views on record.

Des Nilsen seems to have been at war with the authorities since I last saw him. On one occasion he appears to have punched a bully on the nose, but I am not sure if that caused him any trouble. His particular grievance, which I think is entirely justified, is that he is not allowed to publish the music which he has composed and which he is offering to charity. I also took this up strongly with Derek Lewis, who was reconsidering the case when he disappeared from the scene. Des would be happy for me to take it up again with the acting successor.

I was delighted to hear that the Ruth Rendell anthology on murder, to which he has contributed an essay, has appeared. It will be a real help to anyone who wants to know what he is like, particularly when I tell them that he refused a fee because it was 'blood' money.

Brett Mills is a weird man indeed, though full of his own charm. He got rid of all his legal advisors and defended himself for seven weeks in court. He thoroughly enjoyed the experience. He tells me with absolute conviction, 'I won; I proved my innocence.'

Unfortunately for him the jury took a different view and

he is now serving a life sentence for abduction of a girl of twelve, raping her and buggering her. He is by no means convinced that I agree with his account of matters. I told him, however, that in reply to his letter I would have come to visit him even if he was the only prisoner in Whitemoor that I was visiting. He regards me as impotent but, I am glad to think, a good man.

I am also glad to know that he has consented to secure a new solicitor for the purpose of an appeal. I tried to persuade him that a professional can beat an amateur every time in a legal encounter.

Wednesday November 29, 1995

Gave lunch to Geoffrey Walmsley who is writing the official life of the late Fred West. He sat through every moment of Rosemary West's trial and considered that if the jury had been composed of lawyers they might well have acquitted her. He told me that the children were standing by her. They had been brought up to treat the irregularities of the household as normal, but had no idea that the murders were taking place. Geoffrey has not yet met Mrs West, but when he does will let her know what she probably knows already: that, if invited, I shall be happy to visit her. I do not expect this to occur for some time, if indeed it ever does.

Friday December 1, 1995

I visited Brian Vale in Wormwood Scrubs. He is actively intellectual and seems to have plenty of visitors, official and otherwise. I can only offer him supplementary consolation.

Meanwhile the fortunes of Roy have never been far from my mind. When I visited him during the week in the Royal Free Hospital he seemed very cheerful. The chief medical officer at Pentonville and the psychiatrist at the Royal Free, Dr King, who has known him for many years, agree that he is suffering from a mental illness, so he was assuming that it was almost certain that the judge would have to send him to hospital.

Saturday December 2, 1995

Roy rang up in despair to say goodbye. He would be killing himself at the earliest opportunity. Between my seeing him and today he had gone to court. The case was postponed again, but the prospect of prison now loomed large. I tried to ring the prison at once to warn them – failing to get through I rang the Home Office. Later the duty governor at Pentonville rang me to say that he was under fifteen-minute watch, but was 'back to normal'. I am hoping to visit him on Wednesday.

Sunday December 3, 1995

Yesterday one daily newspaper carried a prominent piece which was headed, 'Hindley Will Make West Feel Life is Worth Living, Says Longford'. I am being asked continually if I am going to visit Rosemary West and give the same answer: I have never yet refused to visit a prisoner who requested a visit and I never will. If Rose West wishes to see me I will certainly go.

At the moment of writing, Rose West is in the hospital wing of Durham Prison, as is Myra. Myra broke her leg some time ago, and according to the paper she is being treated for a brittle-bone disorder. I met her new solicitor recently who told me that she was in good form. I hope to receive a birthday card from her this week.

Rose West is being treated, not surprisingly, as a suicide

risk and is widely reported as being very depressed. Her solicitor, however, insists that she is not depressed at all and hopes to move shortly to a normal wing.

This coming week I shall be making five speeches to mark my ninetieth birthday: to the New Bridge party on Monday; at the press launch on Tuesday lunchtime of the paperback of *Avowed Intent*, my most recent volume of autobiography; at my daughter Antonia's party on Tuesday evening; at the Nicko Henderson/Roy Jenkins dinner on Thursday; and at the local party at our Sussex home 'Bernhurst' on Saturday. There is an obvious danger of my turning these occasions into a series of ego trips. I am determined, however, to put some kind of message across.

The best opportunity will occur at the press launch. I have not had such an opportunity for years and I am not likely to have one again. Curiously enough the Rose West drama has given me an unrivalled opportunity to assert my ideal of 'hating the sin and loving the sinner', which has previously been lacking outside the House of Lords. For whatever reason Rose West does not seem to arouse the intense hatred which the tabloid press has taught the public to feel for Myra. Even *The Observer* of today, in a sensible account of Rose West's position, publishes the old Medusa photograph of Myra. They would never dream of publishing a thirty-year-old photograph of anyone else without, at any rate, strong reason.

Thursday December 7, 1995

My daughter Rachel and I repaired to Wandsworth Prison where an opera was being performed in honour of Stephen Tumin. The main parts were taken by professionals, some of the lesser ones by inmates. I was happy once again to run into Derek Lewis.

Friday December 15, 1995

I made yet another visit to Roy in the hospital wing at Pentonville. He was very depressed. He appeared in court on Wednesday and felt that the judge was as hostile to him as ever. He will now go to trial at the Crown Court in February. The only good news is that there will be a different judge. He still entertains hope that in the meanwhile he will be sent back to the Royal Free Hospital.

From talking to someone in his solicitor's office I feel that that is extremely unlikely. Roy is, in his own way, unique and very clever, but unable to make any sensible use of his abilities. He seems to have used several different names in his alleged fraud, that is, the theft of £89,000 from the DSS. At one point it seemed that he actually attempted to pressurise the Minister for Social Security into speeding up the payments.

His moods swing violently between elation and black depression. He says that he will not be alive when the case comes to court. I tell him that it is my duty to do all in my power to make sure that he is.

He is a very articulate man and could, if he chose, write a very good autobiography. He will never do it on his own, but he has agreed that he would allow a 'ghost' to help him. So the ball is in my court. Can I find a 'ghost'? Can I find a publisher? Can I get Home Office permission? Poor Roy!

Sunday December 17, 1995

Another hectic week. One major television appearance, four radio programmes and a speech on penal matters in the House of Lords.

One radio interviewer introduced me thus: 'My next guest is Lord Longford, to talk about Myra Hindley, pornography and Rose West.'

I have not yet found anybody on these programmes to say to my face that Myra ought to stay in prison. I was accused by one friend afterwards of being arrogant in dismissing so-called public opinion. Maybe so. But when you have known somebody for twenty-seven years it is difficult to be patient with a 'man in the street' who only knows what the tabloid press tells him about her.

Once again I am profoundly conscious of the gap between informed opinion and uninformed public emotions. I keep coming back to the taxi driver who told me that he felt cheated of revenge when he heard that Fred West had committed suicide. But he knew that it was wrong to feel that way. I have to accept the fact that feelings similar to those of the taxi driver will always be widely held by the so-called general public.

Those who deal with prisoners at first-hand, the Prison Service and the Probation Service, for example, cannot fail to recognise them as fellow human beings. But to the so-called general public they will always be an alien and even menacing force. It is the business of those who care for humanity and justice to make far more effort than they have made previously to guide the public in the direction of the enlightened taxi driver. It is easy for someone like myself to say we must hate the sin and love the sinner, but it is hard enough to achieve that balance after a lifetime's experience, still more after a moment's reflection.

Wednesday December 20, 1995

The usual call on Roy at Pentonville Hospital. He began by saying goodbye, as he intended to do himself in before Christmas. He is under close supervision so neither of us take this quite seriously. If anything awful happens I suppose that

I shall blame myself, but I am not quite sure what more I could have done.

Roy, with all his faults, has a keen sense of humour. He asks me to deliver a funeral oration when he passes on, but he wants it to be really witty. On the spur of the moment I offered him an ending that amused him. From the pulpit I would say, 'I am optimistic about Roy's future. He has conned me so successfully that he should have no difficulty with St Peter.' He was still laughing when we parted.

Friday December 22, 1995

I set off for Manchester for a Granada programme on Myra Hindley. I was reluctant to leave Elizabeth, though in the end our daughter Judith came down to Bernhurst to spend the night with her. I asked Granada how much they would pay – they said £150. I said call it £1,000 and I might consider it, never thinking that they would agree. They came back and accepted my request.

I was intrigued to learn that they could not find anyone to oppose me on the platform. I did not put this down to my personal prestige, but to the fact that no one, in my recent experience, is ready to stand up on a platform and argue the case against Myra. Large numbers are, of course, happy to denounce her from a sitting position or at a distance.

The audience was self-invited, not representative. It included Winnie Johnson who is the mother of one of the children murdered on the Moors. I began by saying that having visited prisoners for many years I was totally convinced that no prisoner should serve as long as thirty years, let alone life, unless he or she were dangerous. No one for years has supposed that Myra Hindley was dangerous.

The argument between platform and most of the audience resembled the old contest between the man with the trident and the man with the net. I don't know which, on this occasion, was which. No one in the audience argued that Myra was dangerous. No one had ever set eyes on her, but she was a 'hate' figure and as such could not be forgiven.

Next morning I asked myself whether, if I had to do it again, I would do it any better. I concluded that I should have expressed at the beginning (what I took for granted) my profound sympathy for victims and their relatives.

I am left with one or two, though hardly novel, reflections. I am a democrat in the sense that democracy is far superior to any other system. But in regard to prisoners, particularly in view of the remorseless increase in crime (tenfold over the last fifty years), public opinion is liable to be highly emotional.

The public may have their own views about, shall we say, Europe or economic policy without being able to argue on such matters against a professional. But on crime large numbers of the public feel that they know best – to hell with professional opinion. Myra's treatment is just one example of the problem which confronts all with some knowledge of penal matters. How can the government of the day be persuaded to follow the guidance of those who give their lives to these matters? The answer lies with the knowledgeable, who must exert themselves far more strenuously to lighten the darkness of the ignorant.

Wednesday December 27, 1995

To Maidstone to visit once more Winston Silcot. He has been in prison ten years for knifing a man to death but, having obtained three witnesses in his favour, he is hoping to persuade the Home Secretary to let his case go once more to appeal. There seems a long delay at the Home Office. I promised to make contact once more with his solicitor and see if I can be of any service.

The whole scene in which his crime was played out is so far outside my experience that I withhold judgment. Although generally regarded as 'soft on crime' I am at the moment entirely on the side of those who want to take strong measures against the knife culture.

Thursday December 28, 1995

I repaired once more to the hospital wing of Pentonville. My visit to Roy had been confirmed the day before, but on Thursday morning he rang up in an awful state and insisted that I shouldn't come. I told him that I should come regardless.

I rang the very sympathetic chief medical officer. He agreed to see me. The doctor told me that he could not insist on Roy seeing me, but he could take me through the open door of his cell. When I arrived at the cell Roy was in semi-darkness lying on his bed muttering. I went in, gripped him by the hand, and fairly soon had him laughing at some of the old stories.

Friday December 29, 1995

To Belmarsh Prison near Woolwich in south-east London to visit Charlie Bronson, whom I have visited at intervals for about four years. He is considered a most violent man on the prison circuit and is moved round from prison to prison after a month or so. He will go for long periods without violence. Then a sudden rage will overtake him and he will seize and endanger the life of, for example, a governor, a librarian or a prison doctor.

He has been in Broadmoor and Rampton Special Hospitals where they have found him untreatable, yet the prison staff – half a dozen are required to watch him – are obviously fond of him, and he is in a peculiar way a talented writer. He won a Koestler Award for this last year.

On this occasion an impressive lady, a member of the Board of Visitors, joined us, though she in no way insisted on doing so. Her final suggestion to me was very sensible. I should try to make contact with the head of the prison medical service as Charlie is so obviously a medical case.

I should add that for some months he has been engaged to be married to a well-educated lady who has also won a Koestler Award for writing. She was, incidentally, at Moor House Catholic school which was attended earlier by three of my daughters. They became engaged by correspondence without meeting.

I visited her at his request while she was serving a sentence at Holloway for a complicated passport offence. She is appealing against the sentence. I had wondered whether she would proceed with the engagement when she actually met Charlie.

Friday January 19, 1996

I visited David Rundle at Littlehey, near Huntingdon, after quite a long interval. He is still in my view being treated abominably, partly as a result of the unsatisfactory law relating to the recall of life prisoners. While I was waiting to see David I met a leading member of the New Bridge committee who was visiting another life prisoner who had been recalled. In his case the offence was 'pissing' on the platform of a tube station when drunk. He was fined £5 at the time, but he is now back in prison indefinitely. If he had been a discretionary as opposed to a mandatory life prisoner, he, like David, would long ago have been able to go before a tribunal. Not so in his case.

David was recalled eight months ago on the say-so of his local probation officer. This gentleman is now backing efforts made by the chaplain and others to support David's demand to be sent to an open prison for the five years he has left to serve. I should mention that David, once before, spent two years in an open prison without any kind of trouble.

All his reports, I gather, are favourable except that the probation officer in the prison considers that his potential relationships with women are still unsatisfactory. How on earth she can reach this conclusion I cannot imagine.

I promised to write to Minister for Prisons Ann Widdecombe, but first to make contact with this external probation officer who has done David so much harm already, but is now, perhaps, seeking to make reparation.

Reaching Charing Cross on the way back to Bernhurst I was filled with joy when I read that the Maxwell brothers had been cleared of fraud charges connected to the activities of their late father, Robert. I wish that I could say that I made a contribution to this result. I can at least say that I had corresponded encouragingly with Kevin Maxwell, attended for two hours in court to show goodwill, and sent a message of support to Alun Jones, Kevin's wonderful counsel, when the jury retired.

One or two recollections of Bob Maxwell came back to me. I first heard of him when Hugh Gaitskell in 1962 asked me to be chairman of a committee to save the London County Council, then on the point of abolition. I was told that Bob Maxwell, a Labour candidate at the time, would help finance the committee's inquiry. This he did to the tune of £2,000, worth a good deal more then. It enabled us to set up a little office.

Later, when he was in the 'doghouse' having been excluded from the chairmanship of his own company, I was chairing a meeting and saw him in the audience. I went out of my way to say how pleased I was to see my friend there. He remembered this and responded favourably to one or two charitable appeals when he was restored and going strong.

Later again, the *The Mirror* published an article denouncing Myra and, incidentally, myself. I rang up Bob Maxwell as the paper's proprietor and asked whether I could write a reply. He said, 'Go ahead, make it an open letter to me.'

I wrote the open letter and finished with the words, 'Bob, you have won great power by your own exertions. But what is the point of having great power if you use it like a pigmy?'

He rang up: 'Look here, Frank, I've got your piece. It's all right. You haven't got to put in that thing about the pigmy do you?'

I said, 'It is the whole point of the article.'

He said, 'All right, Frank. Have it your own way this time.' The article duly appeared.

Saturday January 20, 1996

Roy rang up in a very disturbed state. He had declined to see me on Thursday on the grounds that he was not very well. On Saturday he told me that he had been upset by the visit of his new QC on Wednesday and had now sacked him. He was also sacking his solicitor. In other words he was behaving like a crazy 'loon'.

I told him that he was pursuing a 'high risk' policy. This might be one way of demonstrating that he really was 'bonkers', but I couldn't feel that it would work out best for him.

I rang up the duty governor immediately afterwards, asking that the suicide watch should be restored. The duty governor rang back afterwards. He had been to see Roy and taken any steps available. I told Roy, who kept repeating that he wanted to die alone, that I would never desert him. I should be coming to the prison as soon as the chief medical officer could see me and would hope, as on the last occasion, to see Roy. As usual Roy cheered up even as we talked. The case for transferring him into hospital is overwhelming, but between you and me he should be under careful supervision, though not, repeat not, in handcuffs.

Wednesday February 7, 1996

I visited Wormwood Scrubs and saw two prisoners serving life sentences. Brian Vale was as voluble and as friendly as ever.

The other, Uday Narayan, told me a strange story indeed. He is serving a life sentence for allegedly murdering his daughter-in-law. He lived alone, but she visited him from time to time. She vanished suddenly. He assumed she was with her boyfriend, but after several years her body was discovered under his house.

He appears to have 'sacked' one or two solicitors, which in my experience seldom works. He was left to defend himself at the trial, but is now trying to get legal help with his appeal. I shall continue to keep in touch with him. He comes from Fiji which may not have helped him with a British jury, as his manner of speaking might have put them off.

Friday February 9, 1996

I made my way to Snaresbrook where Roy's case was coming once more before a judge, still without a jury. On this occasion he was equipped with a QC, a junior counsel and his faithful solicitor. Legal aid must have been drawn on plentifully. The mental evidence pointed to the conclusion that he should be given psychiatric treatment in hospital.

I had to leave before lunch, but Roy rang me in the evening to say that victory had for once come his way. The courts seem to have said goodbye to him – handing him over to the medical authorities at the Royal Free Hospital.

More than once in recent weeks he has talked of wanting to be left alone to die. Not so on this occasion. He was highly elated. I don't grudge him a dose of happiness, whether or not short-lived. I shall be visiting him tomorrow in Pentonville before he moves.

Wednesday February 21, 1996

I called on Des Nilsen at Whitemoor. The visit was mainly remarkable for the horrifying delays. He was friendly to me as always nowadays, but very hostile to the prison authorities. Even a saint, which he is far from being, would have plenty to complain about.

In the first place, as he has told me before, he is prohibited from sending out his musical compositions; in the second place, under some new ruling, he has to decide whether to have a typewriter or a keyboard in his cell. He is not allowed to have both. In other words he can write, or he can compose music. One or the other.

I shall now take both matters up again with the acting director-general of the Prison Service and ask for an interview with him or a deputy. The trouble is that Des writes me letters which are so offensive to the authorities that I can't pass them on. I must do the best I can.

There is good news on the Myra front. The Parole Board has agreed that she should be allowed to go to an open prison. This is usually taken as a sign that the prisoner is on the way out after a certain period has elapsed. I have not yet learnt whether Myra wants to go or indeed whether her leg injury would make it feasible. But it is very encouraging all the same.

Friday February 23, 1996

I visited Roy in the Royal Free. He was vehemently protesting because, for the first time, he was not in a room by himself, but in a ward of eight noisy youngsters, all presumably mental in one way or another. He was already talking about trying to get back to prison and, failing that, of escaping. He promised to do nothing while I made enquiries.

Saturday February 24, 1996

Roy rang up in desperation and announced that he was being harassed by the young companions, one of them at least armed with a cosh. I got on to the acting manager of the hospital who visited and reported later that the implement, whose nature remains unclear to me, had now been sent away. Apparently there is no single room available. Roy rang later, somewhat calmer, gratified by the attention paid him. So it goes on.

Friday March 1, 1996

I visited Roy, now back in the Royal Free Hospital. He was in a ward, but it was not a dormitory; it was more like an alcove. No one could look in on him, but his neighbour was all too audible through the compartment wall.

For the first time I fully understood how frightful it would be to have someone playing loud music all day long through this compartment wall.

As always, Roy was subject to exceptional mood swings. Very irritated with me at the beginning because I was not ready to sign something about accommodation after he was released from custody. But when I agreed, full of gratitude, over-laudatory and as always full of humour.

Friday March 8, 1996

I spoke to Myra on the telephone. She spoke slowly and very clearly, like someone in a responsible position, so I suppose that her cause has become just that in her life. It is espoused by so many others that I should not be surprised if that was so. She was very friendly.

I reminded her that on my ninetieth birthday she had written to me comparing me to Robbie Ross. Robbie, it will be remembered, gravely raised his hat to Oscar Wilde as the latter with bowed head and manacled legs moved away after conviction.

I am glad that she is coming out into the open at every opportunity. My dear friend, my oldest friend, David Astor, once editor of *The Observer*, was, I think, always opposed to this policy, but I am quite sure that keeping her head down will leave her at the mercy of the tabloids for ever.

I was very glad that she wrote a major article in *The Guardian*. She told me that she had written an article for the Oxford University Law Society, an undergraduate body. This is to be splashed across the front page of the *Sunday Telegraph*. She tells me that she is also writing an article for *Cosmopolitan* which I suppose is a daring woman's paper. All to the good.

Sunday March 17, 1996

For the first time for ages I did not visit a prison this week. I had a cold which did not prevent me from going to the House of Lords, but I postponed visits to Roy in the Royal Free Hospital and Des Nilsen and Eddie Richardson in Whitemoor.

Wednesday March 27, 1996

I visited Roy at the Royal Free Hospital. He was in one of his despondent moods, working off his feelings on me. He had, however, at last done what I had begged him to do for so long. He had written an account (half a dozen pages) of what he considered had made him a thief and later a conman throughout his adult life. It may be that the effort of analysing himself had left him shaken. (On Saturday evening I read it to Elizabeth who thought that it was very well written and very perceptive. I rang Roy and got Elizabeth to speak to him. He was overjoyed to receive her opinion. It could be a turning point if he could somehow or other establish himself as some kind of writer. He will have to begin with telling the story of his own very painful life history.)

Friday March 29, 1996

I saw Tony Wolf, aged twenty-seven, in Pentonville Prison. He is facing a fraud charge, and the possibility of six years in prison, though he still has some hope of being sent, like Roy, to a mental hospital. In my long experience of prisoners I have met few who have been treated quite so harshly by life.

He came into the world when an American soldier raped his mother. As a small child he was buggered by several friends or boyfriends of his mother. He was a truant from school and would appear to have had little or no formal education. He had, however, written to me a long, coherent letter and he talked well and lucidly about his life.

His life had, in fact, been one of fraud and conmanship. He has been in prison or on probation since boyhood, and now he is faced with further charges for obtaining up to £71,000 by fraud.

Visiting him in the same prison as Roy, I found myself making inevitable comparisons. As Tony is only twenty-seven and Roy is fifty, the former seems to have more chance of becoming a normal citizen than the latter. On the other hand, Roy would appear to have a gift of writing, not possessed by Tony to the same extent.

I should add two further facts about Tony's sad history.

When in Leyhill Open Prison in Gloucestershire he was buggered by two prisoners. Today in Pentonville, he is segregated on rule 43 for his own protection because he is regarded as a 'grass' by other prisoners. The only hopeful thing he told me was that, though not a Catholic, he established at one point a good relationship with a Catholic priest, now abbot of Ealing Abbey. I have promised to get in touch with the abbot, and also a therapist.

He was very anxious that I should give evidence at his trial. I said that I would like to do so, but only if the counsel thought that it would be useful. I would try to be present in any case, though it would take place in that horribly remote Snaresbrook court. I would need to be given some kind of assurance that if I went there I would not spend as many fruitless hours as when I attended more than one of Roy's hearings.

Wednesday April 3, 1996

The new White Paper on prisons by Michael Howard was published just before a statement was made on his behalf in the House of Lords by Emily Blatch. It carried further the proposals which he outlined at the Conservative party conference last autumn. Jack Straw in the Commons failed to condemn it sufficiently.

I should say at this point that Howard's wife motored me back to London recently after my old Cabinet colleague Douglas Jay's funeral. I assured her that there was nothing personal in the criticisms of her husband so widely ventilated among those with any knowledge of prisons or prisoners at first-hand.

I wrote not long ago to Tony Blair himself. I appreciated his passionate desire, which of course I share, to win the election, but I recalled the words of the poet Crosland, friend of Oscar Wilde, who wrote:

I trod the road to hell
But there were things I might have sold
And did not sell.

I got back a friendly but very unhelpful reply.

I told the House the White Paper was 'an evil document'. Fifty years' experience of the Lords has taught me that the one thing they hate is an unpleasant personal atmosphere. It is easier for us to avoid it than for the Commons because the top ministers, apart from the Lord Chancellor, are in the lower house.

I made everyone happy to start with by describing Emily Blatch as 'the angel of light employed to speak on behalf of the prince of darkness'. After that no one seemed to mind the savagery of my remarks, whose essence they are familiar with by now.

Friday April 5, 1996

I made my way to Latchmere House, the resettlement prison where nearly half the inmates work outside. I had visited it twice before, and picked it out in a speech in the House of Lords as the best prison known to me, admittedly with a selected intake.

The new governor was impressive. I asked him, for example, whether prisoners called him by his Christian name. He said that he permitted it, but did not encourage it.

Wednesday April 10, 1996

Visited Roy at the Royal Free yesterday and was allowed to take him out to lunch at a nearby pub. It all went very well. He saw me to the tube and then walked back to the hospital. He told me that that was in order, but I suppose I was unwise to let him go back alone.

In the evening Roy rang up to say that when he left me at the tube he was accosted by a reporter from *The Star* newspaper. Later I was rung up by *The Star* so the thing had actually happened, which is not always the case with Roy's reportage. I rang the hospital warning them that they might be rung by *The Star*, and complaining that some 'mole' in the hospital must have leaked it.

Today the excellent Dr King, Roy's psychiatrist, rang me to reproach me gently for accusing a member of his staff of leaking the event. I said that I didn't see who else could have done it. He pointed out that Roy might have 'blabbed' to *The Star* himself.

I offered to apologise, but he said not to bother. I still think that it was a mole in the hospital, but it is quite true that Roy babbles away to journalists.

Today I visited Blantyre House in Kent, usually referred to as, but not officially I think, a resettlement prison. Only 20 out of 100 work outside compared with 65 out of 150 at Latchmere.

The prisoners are selected with extreme care. Everyone calls everyone by their Christian name and the atmosphere is one of genuine friendship.

Every now and then, but very seldom, someone has to be sent away. There are very strict rules against violence, drugs or alcohol. I would like to think that there could be several Blantyres or Latchmeres. But I do realise that the conditions are exceptional.

The prisoner I was visiting was Eric Jasper. Many years ago he escaped from jail with Ronnie Biggs, though not himself a train robber. He lived in Australia for seven years. Biggs moved over to South America, but Eric Jasper was collared by the police and finished his sentence in England.

For a number of years he made a respectable income in lorry transport, but eventually a large consignment of cannabis was found in his lorry; the source and recipient of the lorry load were not prosecuted, but Eric (who still insists that he is innocent) got ten years in prison.

I have, on one occasion, entertained at lunch in the House of Lords a very agreeable and very loyal wife, his daughter, who has a good job in the Post Office, and his granddaughter who has won a scholarship to a private school.

What Eric values most is being able to roam at large within the prison perimeter. Very different from being shut in a cell, or under close supervision throughout the day. What he objects to most, along with staff and prisoners alike, is the new Howardite rule that you can't get home leave until after six months. Howard is clearly as unpopular with the staff here as in the rest of the prisons.

Wednesday April 17, 1996

Called on Crispin Allen at Wandsworth. A strange man by any standards, but attractive and intelligent. An old Etonian, he travelled the world for ten years after leaving school, picking up a living as he went. At one point he got married, but it seems that that has more or less come to an end.

He went to a party, was invited back to the house of some unmarried lady, indeed, into the bedroom. He readily admits to having had sex with her, but it was not until four months later that she reported him for rape. He is now doing a sentence of five years.

When I first met him he had hair down to his shoulders. It is slightly shorter now. In Wandsworth, he has qualified as a photographer and seems to feel that when he emerges from prison he will be able to make quite a living. But he has been refused parole partly, it seems, because he has not been ready to participate in the group-therapy sessions for sex offenders.

He hopes to emerge from prison in any case next

January, but there may be some restrictions on his movements. It is unfortunate for him that his mother still lives in the same small town as his victim.

He has told me more than once that my visits to him do him no good with the staff. This happens every now and then to me in my prison visiting.

Later I gave tea at the House of Lords to four prison officers from the Oxford prison where I began my own prison visiting in the late 1930s.

Wednesday May 1, 1996

I visited Billy Crittenden in Wandsworth. He has moved around a good deal since I last saw him in Maidstone. He is doing a sentence of six years for rape. It sounds like one of these marginal cases, though I cannot suppose that he comes out of it well.

He is a gypsy and is married to a charming wife who is standing by him and has been to tea with me in the House of Lords. But he was, admittedly, having sex with another gypsy girl. It is claimed on her behalf that she resisted his sexual advances when she discovered he was married. As to that, I have no opinion but, I repeat, his wife and father are standing by him which is a good sign.

I cannot understand why he has been moved from prison to prison except that he appears to be a troublemaker in the eyes of the prison authorities. He says that it is due to the fact that in a fit of depression he slit his wrists, which are certainly very swollen. On the face of it he has a genuine grievance. I promised to do what I could. He is an endearing character.

Friday May 3, 1996

I was persuaded by Andrew McCooey to visit a woman called Marie or Maria Pearson (she is happy to be called either) in

Bulwood Hall Women's Prison in Essex. She is one of his clients. She has been in prison for ten years and is serving a life sentence for murder.

Andrew seems hopeful, however, that with the help of new psychiatric evidence, the Home Office will be persuaded to send her case back to the Appeal Court. It is hoped that there may be a verdict of manslaughter with diminished responsibility.

Middle-aged, she is still beautiful and has a poignant story to tell. Not long after her child was born by her second husband (she had two children by an earlier one) her husband's new mistress began taunting her unbearably. She said that she was going to go off with the husband and take away the child. Maria stabbed her seventeen times.

A human tragedy but, at the same time, a very difficult case for lawyers and psychiatrists to sort out. She is probably a difficult prisoner from the point of view of the authorities. She is not ready to accept the terms of work on offer, and, though a Catholic, prefers the Anglican chaplain.

She is desperately anxious to move back to Cookham Wood Prison in Kent to be near her daughter.

Friday May 10, 1996

I repaired to Whitemoor yet again. I must have referred earlier to the new regulations. I think the silliest of all is being searched yet again when one has visited the toilets, although a prison officer was stationed outside. I find it increasingly difficult not to denounce all these restrictions to prison officers who mostly sympathise with me, but are nevertheless somewhat embarrassed by my remarks.

I was very anxious to discover from Eddie Richardson exactly what steps, if any, I could take to help him. He has been treated abominably since getting his extravagant sentence (twenty-five years for alleged importation of drugs). Three times he has been moved for a month on mysterious security grounds – to Liverpool, Bristol (where I visited him) and Durham.

He is still retained not only in category A, but in 'high-risk' category A. After seven years of impeccable conduct in prison he is approaching a time when, in theory, he will be eligible for parole, but this will be impossible if he is still in 'high-risk' category A.

He feels that Whitemoor is a hostile place for him and is desperately anxious to be moved. He wants to go to Long Lartin in Worcestershire which, however, isn't quite ready for prisoners in his category.

I have been in touch with the head of the Prison Service about Eddie, who rather grudgingly has agreed for me to see a certain Mr Wheatley again. I expect to be met with a blank wall, but I must have another go. Eddie does not wish me to go public on his behalf. In my experience that is the only way to overcome a confirmed bureaucratic resistance.

With no justification, as far as I am aware, they have got it into their heads, in a kind of inverted compliment to him, (a) that he is the mastermind of many of the troubles in Whitemoor, and (b) that he has powerful criminal associates outside and large sums tucked away abroad. This makes him a major escape risk. In my eyes all total nonsense. And not very nice nonsense at that.

Des Nilsen is absorbed in his autobiography. I would imagine that if he were a free man and told his tale frankly, it would be a big seller. I have tried for quite a while to get the ban lifted on the 'export' of his musical compositions. This has now been lifted, but another restriction prevents him having a typewriter and a keyboard in his cell at the same time.

Friday May 24, 1996

My daughter Rachel and I visited David Rundle and a lifers' group in Littlehey in Huntingdon. Rachel is writing a novel in which someone figures who is recalled to prison in the same kind of way as David.

I spent an hour there. Halfway through Rachel and David adjourned. She found him very helpful.

I suppose that it was rather unusual to be addressing twelve men convicted of murder. I don't think anyone, however sharp-sighted, would have noticed any difference between them and a dozen so-called ordinary people. The only question which surprised me was whether the Queen could intervene to prevent the enormities of Howardism. I had to dispel the illusion.

One somewhat elderly gentleman had been in prison since 1957, longer than anyone I know personally, but I am told there is someone still in prison after forty-four years. In such prolonged cases of incarceration the explanation is usually either that the prisoner has made many attempts to escape, or that he has been recalled after an interval (as has David).

This gentleman said that he was out of custody from 1984 until 1989, but he was recalled because he had helped a friend to commit suicide. I would obviously need to explore the matter more thoroughly before offering an opinion.

He seemed such a gentle type, but I am afraid that appearance proves nothing.

I will mention one other bit of dialogue at the prison. There was a long delay as usual. The officers at the gate had not been properly informed, as so often, about our visit. A thick wall of glass separated the officers from the visitors, and there was not, as at Pentonville for instance, a special gadget in the wall to facilitate communication.

Becoming a little testy as the officer and I shouted at each other, I said that we would become better friends if it wasn't for this horrible glass barrier. He replied, 'You have never had a knife at your throat.' That started quite a train of thought, though it did not provide justification in my eyes for the glass barrier.

Undoubtedly a prison officer in the course of his service may find himself threatened by a dangerous criminal. Does this produce a mentality in prison which spreads not only to prisoners in general, but to visitors?

Sunday May 26, 1996

Roy rang up to say that he is being discharged in three weeks. Good news or not? I can't help thinking that there will be a bit of a press outcry if it happens as soon as that; after all, he has pleaded guilty to stealing many thousands of pounds from the DSS.

He was supposed to go into the Royal Free to receive treatment. We shall be told that no such miraculous cure has been effected since Ernest Sanders was released from prison because of senility, and was very soon out and about, ready for business.

Thursday May 30, 1996

I called on Brian Vale, a fascinating man who is admittedly excitable. We had a very interesting discussion about the place of remorse in the lives of prisoners. I enjoy talking to him immensely, when I can get a word in. I agree with him that he has learnt a lot about himself since he has been in prison.

Monday June 3, 1996

I gave lunch to Vice-Admiral Sir Peter Woodhead, the prisons' ombudsman. He had made public already his disquiet at the restriction on his powers recently introduced by Michael Howard. My daughter Rachel joined us. It was a pleasure to find that he already knew about her as a fellow worker in the penal field.

He revealed himself as a committed Christian which, in practice, means that he is an opponent of Howardism.

Tuesday June 4, 1996

I went to Norwich to give a talk on forgiveness to an enthusiastic meeting arranged by a Christian organisation which provides counsellors to those with problems.

I spent the night with an impressive Christian couple. The husband is a soldier and merchant banker by profession. The wife is the head of the counselling organisation.

They told me many things bearing on forgiveness. One of the most interesting was that my hostess had recently counselled three prison officers who had become fearful in recent times. I am not quite clear whether this was because of a shortage of staff, or a new hostility among prisoners. Either way it belonged directly to the age of Howardism.

I had told the meeting, somewhat rashly, that I had never had occasion to forgive anybody. Next morning, I was due to take part in a television programme on the Conservative party. I was duly met at Liverpool Street, but the driver had no instructions except to drop me at St Paul's.

In the event half an hour was wasted while we tried to locate the organisers of the programme. When they eventually turned up, I was in a state of annoyance and was admitting to myself that for the first time I felt that there was someone whom I ought to forgive. Rationally or otherwise, I realised that I should not be happy until I had obtained an apology. When the organisers arrived, an apology was indeed offered, but somewhat reluctantly.

I learnt two lessons as a result. One, that most of us when badly treated feel this strange need for an apology. Two, that most of us when bound to apologise do it with reluctance.

Curiously enough my dear friend, Jenny Macgillikin, a very high-minded woman, had told me the day before how hurt she had been by the conduct of one of her friends, who had become jealous of another of Jenny's friends. She couldn't forgive her until she had had an apology. It all sounds very petty, but is also sadly human.

Friday June 7, 1996

I repaired to Belmarsh Prison near Woolwich to see my old friend Charlie Bronson. The first time I met him I was told that he was the most violent man in the prison. Was I ready to go into his cell alone? I had no option except to chance it.

I went in and asked him what he had been doing that day. He said, 'Two thousand press ups.' I said, 'I used to do a dozen a day. I'll see if I can do one now.' I went down on the floor and with some difficulty did one. We have been friends ever since.

He is full of fun and, in a strange way, talent. Though a man without formal education he won a Koestler Award last year and is having a book published this September. But he flies into unaccountable rages and has taken more than one governor as hostage.

On this occasion I was told with some embarrassment that he did not feel like seeing me. The governor of the prison, who takes a personal interest, came down to see me and explained that Charlie had not turned against me, but did not wish me to see him in his present state of fury. The governor, a man full of human understanding, is doing all for him that seems possible.

I am writing to Charlie immediately to say that I respect

him for his reason for not wanting to see me. I shall also suggest reviewing his book. One would say that he is unique, except that there are many individual prisoners who, like him, do not fall into any category.

Friday June 14, 1996

To Highdown, Surrey, to see Mark Tomlinson. He has served in fifteen prisons. I have been informed by governors that in effect he is a troublesome prisoner, though there is no allegation of violence against staff.

Mark threw a little more light on his reputation. He was indignant, understandably, that he was moved from Latchmere House, the resettlement prison, after three anonymous fellow prisoners had complained about him.

He told me that, for example, on one occasion he was offered his pay in what seems an insulting fashion. He told the prison officer concerned that he could keep it.

I told him that President Nixon might have sympathised with him. At the moment of his disgrace he announced, 'I've screwed everything up. I've let everyone down, but I am not going to grovel.' If he, Mark Tomlinson, wanted to play it that way, it was up to him. But he must expect unpleasant consequences. He took this with a good grace.

Wednesday June 26, 1996

I visited Tony Wolf who has been moved to Wormwood Scrubs. His situation reminds me of Roy. Both have pleaded guilty to extensive frauds. Both were in Pentonville and, in each case, personality disorder has been diagnosed. But there the resemblance ends.

Roy is fifty-one, Tony twenty-seven. Tony is heterosexual, Roy the opposite. Both are highly intelligent, but Roy has shown a literary ability which Tony has not, so far at least. Tony is determined to turn over a new leaf and lead an honest life.

I suggested to him that he would benefit from counselling of one kind or another. He told me that he would become a Mormon, which is an obvious handicap in the search for a counsellor. One can't expect Wormwood Scrubs to lay on a Mormon chaplain. It happens, however, that Bob Tierney, an ex-prisoner, but now training to be a probation officer, is also a Mormon with a Mormon wife. So perhaps Bob will be able to help Tony.

Wednesday July 3, 1996

Visited Brian Vale and Uday Narayan at Wormwood Scrubs. Nothing extraordinary. What sticks in my mind is the extraordinary defensiveness of the Prison Service when they make even a slight error. I was told that Narayan would be in court all week, but on Wednesday morning I had a letter from him that made it plain that this was not so. I asked for the deputy governor to arrange for me to see him after all. The young woman who answered was very defiant.

Friday July 5, 1996

What I would call an historic day in the Lords. For the first time an archbishop of Canterbury launched a major debate in the House, initiating what the papers unanimously called 'a moral crusade'. He was speaking to a motion on the role of schools in promoting society's moral responsibilities. When he sat down I was rather disappointed. His references to Christianity were far from explicit. He said himself that he realised that he was not speaking from a pulpit.

I shall pluck up courage and hope to tell him that the pulpit is where bishops speak from most effectively. But since reading the press yesterday and today I have revised my opinion. I think that he has struck a great blow for morals, if only by arousing the sleeping conscience of a nation.

Sunday July 7, 1996

The *News of the World*'s first leader today is headed 'Brady's Crazy Tapes for Kids'. The article begins, 'Ian Brady, that most evil of child murderers, has found himself a new therapy in the secure hospital for the criminally insane where he is detained. He records audio tapes for blind children. The idea is that this small and woefully late contribution to the welfare of young people will help with his "condition".'

I really cannot understand – though I suppose I ought to – why a really nice man like Phil Hall, the editor of the *News of the World*, who took me to lunch at the Gay Hussar on Tuesday and spoke of his desire for his to be a 'moral paper', can be responsible for such nauseating stuff. In the first place it must be presumed that what Ian Brady is doing is helpful to blind children. No one who is not what the *News of the World* would call criminally insane would say that that was wrong. But, in the second place, is it right – it obviously is – that the hospital should find a form of atonement that is also therapeutic for Ian Brady?

Many years ago he offered his kidney, which was rejected. I am glad he is in such enlightened hands. After I visited him for many years he turned against me. It must have been hard for him to hear me saying so often that he, not Myra, was the architect of the Moors murders. But I was very happy to receive a friendly card from him on my ninetieth birthday.

Tuesday July 9, 1996

Went up to Belsize Park where Roy is now installed in a flat and gave him lunch in a nearby pub. The news about him is marginally better. He has gone to see the social services person whom I telephoned. This person has arranged for him to see someone who seems nearer to finding him employment. But not until August. I am watching community care in operation closely and suspiciously.

Thursday July 11, 1996

Brixton, in my experience, has always been an overcrowded remand prison. The remand part of it is still overcrowded, with prisoners spending, I gather, up to twenty-three hours a day in their cells.

There are also a number of sentenced prisoners and a 'lifers' unit there, in which life seems relatively good. My friend William Close is one of the few prisoners whom I have visited over the years and about whose innocence I am certain. In many cases I don't make up my mind, and in still more cases the guilty prisoner is being treated very badly. But William Close and a friend are doing life sentences for murder, and I feel sure that they didn't commit it.

His mother, whom I have met, was badly beaten up by a 'partner' who had a criminal record. She was taken unconscious to hospital. The partner was then found murdered. William and his friend were convicted in spite of the judge summing up favourably. His QC called it a 'freak' jury decision and so it seems it was.

If his sentence is confirmed he will be sent off to Gartree Prison in Market Harborough, Leicestershire, a very long way from his mother, with his alleged accomplice going to Wormwood Scrubs. I told him that I would gladly fight this allocation if necessary, but naturally hoped for the best from the appeal.

Friday July 12, 1996

I went to Highdown in Surrey to visit, yet again, Mark Tomlinson, who is serving five years for armed robbery, having previously served seven for the same offence. He is very intelligent, except about himself.

He is the first prisoner whom I have ever met who said that he might prefer serving his full time in prison to going to a YMCA hostel if that were the condition imposed on him at his release. There is something reckless about him, or happy-go-lucky to use a kinder word.

He would like to become a counsellor and, with that in mind, studies as an external student at Goldsmith's College in the evening. I can imagine him being a helpful counsellor to a certain kind of client, but I have to admit to being anxious about his future on release.

Wednesday July 24, 1996

Visited Charlie Bronson in Belmarsh. For the first time there were no staff outside the door while I visited him. He has been promised a curious reward of two years in Broadmoor if his progress continues.

I think that it was on his last visit to Broadmoor that he spent some time on the roof and did a lot of damage.

His humour can be difficult to appreciate. Some time ago I visited a lady of good family who had been to a Catholic school attended earlier by one of my daughters. She had actually become engaged to him on the strength of his published poems although she had never met him. I was not surprised to find that the engagement did not survive their first encounter. He described it to me in this way: 'She said to me, "You have two front teeth missing"' (he had lost them in an earlier prize fight). 'I said to her, "If you say that again I'll knock out yours."'

It is hard to convey the genial smile with which he told me this story. The phrase a 'funny-man' may have been coined to describe him. But his great strength makes him rather terrifying.

I had an unusual experience on the way up. The kindly governor was escorting me down a corridor when a bell rang and six prison officers rushed past us. 'An incident', the governor remarked coolly and led me to the gate. But for half an hour we were unable to leave the prison while 'the incident' was cleared up.

Eventually the governor escorted me to the taxi remarking as he did so, 'I have to be searched again when I go in.' Bureaucracy run mad surely, though the governor would probably say that he was rightly subjected to the same interferences as the staff.

Saturday July 27, 1996

Newspapers full of the decision by Michael Howard to allow the case of the Bridgewater Four to go back again to the Appeal Court. Their conviction for the murder of newspaper boy Carl Bridgewater is to be re-examined. My own memories of that sad story are quite vivid.

Not so long after the convictions, I was visiting Ian Brady, then in Gartree Prison. Anne Whelan, mother of Michael Hickey, just seventeen at the time of his conviction as one of the Bridgewater Four, was standing outside the prison addressing her son on the roof. 'Come down Mickey,' she kept crying out.

I joined in the cry. But he stayed up there for nine days which affected his mental state considerably.

Later when I visited Ian Brady in Ashworth Special Hospital, Michael Hickey was a fellow patient. I remember him telling me how anxious he was to rejoin his friends in prison.

The reference back to the Appeal Court is yet one more triumph for Edward Fitzgerald, whom I like to refer to as my grandson though he is, strictly speaking, a grandson-in-law. I rang up to congratulate him. I was pleased to hear that Anne Whelan referred to my kindness in the earlier years of her son's imprisonment. I am sitting down now to write a warm message of congratulations.

Wednesday July 31, 1996

Visited Billy Crittenden at Canterbury Prison. Left home at 9.20 a.m., walked to Etchingham station. Reached Canterbury at 1.20 p.m. Into the prison by 2 p.m.

Was annoyed to find that I was stationed in the visiting room at a table within two yards of the presiding officers. I complained that usually my visits were not supervised. They told me that there was a reason which I would discover.

When Billy arrived I learnt that he was in what he called the punishment block – 'banged up' for twenty-three hours a day. This was for his own protection. I have since written to the governor to ask whether there could be any justification for treating a prisoner in this way. Billy insists that there is no need for protection whatever. He is admittedly a rapist, which is unpopular in prisons, but there is a vulnerable prisoners' wing. This solitary confinement has no justification whatever.

Trying to understand how the prison could have got it so wrong, I could only learn that he has exchanged insults with a 'mate' who had just been convicted of murder. I am not quite sure who spoke first, but Billy shouted across the yard, 'You old murderer,' and his mate retorted, 'You old rapist, I'll get you.' There the matter rests until I hear from the governor.

Friday August 2, 1996

Visited Whitemoor in Cambridgeshire. Even more than the usual trouble getting in. Visits nominally begin at 2 p.m. I arrived at 1.30 but did not get in until 2.10. Even then I only got in by walking across to the prison without being summoned.

The ladies at the visiting centre are quite charming and very sympathetic. On this occasion while I was kept waiting they rang up the prison and were told that there was a problem.

Eddie Richardson, when I saw him, said he had heard that I was at the centre some time before I got into the prison. He thinks that the staff are against all do-gooders, including myself. Once again I am going to write to the governor, not to express my irritation, but to try to make sure that I get adequate time with Eddie Richardson and Des Nilsen when I visit Whitemoor. I usually go on a Friday when the House of Lords is not sitting. I catch an eleven o'clock train to Peterborough, wait half an hour to catch a branch-line train to March, where I have a drink and a sandwich before going to the prison. I am hard put in the end to catch a six o'clock train at Charing Cross to get me to Etchingham in time for dinner at Bernhurst.

Eddie and Des were much the same as usual. Two strong personalities: Eddie, very normal; Des, very strange. As previously reported I have taken up Eddie's continued high-risk categorisation with the prisons' ombudsman. Eddie is in correspondence with someone in his office, but was very grateful for any suggestion that I would try to see someone there personally.

On the last occasion Des was very anxious that he should be allowed visits from a former television newsreader, Gordon Honeycombe, who is going to help Eddie. Since then he has been allowed the visits, for which I suppose I deserve some credit.

But Des is having a lot of trouble with the solicitor who is now in physical possession of the manuscript of his autobiography. I offered to intervene but he did not wish it at this stage.

Friday August 9, 1996

Visited David Rundle at Littlehey Prison in Huntingdon. By now I know not to tell the first taxi driver who transports me that I understand that this is John Major country, though the Prime Minister lives close by and is well-liked locally. I have been told before now that he is a Brixton man. Their hero, understandably, is Oliver Cromwell who was born in Huntingdon in a house pointed out as we proceed to Littlehey.

I could write a whole book about the treatment of David Rundle since his recall to prison. I have, in fact, asked one question about him in the House of Lords and interviewed the then Minister for Prisons, Michael Forsyth. One day I am sure that the treatment of life prisoners on recall will be radically improved, even though an amendment I once moved with that in mind got nowhere at the time.

David Rundle, whom I have now known for sixteen years, killed his wife after a domestic row. He served thirteen years for the crime. When he was released he was advised not to consort with a certain lady. He failed to follow the instruction, but found the lady an unsatisfactory partner and ended the relationship. She then accused him of harassing her.

After a year of freedom, therefore, he was recalled to prison on the say-so of a probation officer. He has now been in prison during this second spell for two and a half years without coming before any court or panel. If he had been a discretionary instead of a mandatory life prisoner he would have been able to appear before a panel with proper representation.

The last time the Parole Board looked at his case they recommended an open prison for him, but for reasons unknown he was sent to Littlehey. There have not been many signs of the promised treatment. The Parole Board considered his case afresh in June this year, but now it is August and nothing has been heard from them.

I told him that I would write to his wing governor without much expectation of a satisfactory explanation for his treatment. I expect to be approaching the prisons' ombudsman about David in the near future.

During the week I had a telephone conversation with the very helpful governor of Canterbury Prison. I had written to him complaining that Billy Crittenden was being kept twenty-three hours a day in his cell, apparently for his own protection. He told me that Billy Crittenden's reading of the situation is not correct. He is not being kept in seclusion for his own protection, but because of his conduct. He insists on shouting insults at another prisoner, recently convicted of murder, against whom Billy, according to the governor, gave crucial evidence at his trial.

According to Billy, as I have already recorded, the exchanges were jocular, but they do not seem so to the authorities in the prison. The governor is anxious for him to be transferred back to Wandsworth.

Billy strongly objects to this. One reason is that one of the prison officers at Wandsworth is a brother-in-law of the girl Billy was convicted of raping.

Sunday August 25, 1996

Visits this week to Charlie Bronson, my friend of five years' standing, and a prisoner new to me, Eric Yates. I like to believe that all my visits are, in some slight degree, of value to prisoners. But some are much more interesting than others from my point of view. These two rank well by that standard.

Charlie Bronson, in spite of, or maybe because of, the fact that he is regarded as the most difficult man in prison, is undeniably popular with prison staff. When I arrived at Belmarsh this time, the gate officer behind the usual glass wall became quite jolly. 'Oh! You want to see Charlie,' he said, and soon I was ushered in to the presence. There have been times when eleven prison officers were stationed outside his prison cell, presumably in case he might kidnap me.

But this time he was surrounded by a friendly group including a female governor and a female educationalist. The latter was teaching him how to use a word processor on which he was spilling out a new book on physical fitness.

On this subject he can speak with some authority. I have recorded before now that he does 2,500 press-ups a day, but on September 1 he hopes to make new history and set a world record for the number of press-ups performed with a man on his back. This is no fantasy. Permission has been given, and I was introduced to the prison officer, a physical training instructor, who will play his part in the act.

Charlie was very anxious that I should attend the ceremony, but it coincides with Elizabeth's ninetieth birthday party. In a way I am rather relieved not to be able to be present.

On Friday I repaired to Gartree where there are, I believe, about three hundred lifers. I had a long talk with Eric Yates, but William Close, the second prisoner whom I had hoped to see, did not wish for a visit.

I left him what I hope was a friendly note. I told him that he was not the first Gartree prisoner who had declined to see me. Years earlier I visited Ian Brady several times in that prison, playing some part in his eventual transfer to Ashworth Special Hospital. There came a time, however, when he not only cut off communication but, according to one newspaper, referred to me as a 'Home Office lackey'.

Eric Yates is a grey-haired man of sixty-five. One would not be surprised to find him about to retire from successfully managing a local shop, though he was a security guard. Mrs Wing, governor of Holloway Prison, once said of Myra Hindley, 'Myra is no criminal.' No one looks less like a criminal than Eric Yates.

He had sent me three typewritten pages in which he argued very lucidly what sounded like a simple case. He had committed manslaughter, killing a female partner in a row, although it was apparently admitted that he had no intention of killing her. He received a tariff from the Home Secretary of three years, but has already spent six in prison with no time set yet for release. The Parole Board, meeting in 1995, seemed to feel for some unspecified reason that he was not yet ready for it.

I was interested at once, if only because of the strong conviction and lucidity with which he expressed himself.

I am old enough, however, to be aware that there is always some explanation, even if not a good one, for what appears to be unfair treatment. Sure enough, his life story was extraordinary. When he was fifteen he was convicted of theft (a minor one he assured me) and sent to Rampton Special Hospital, of all places, where he spent no less than twelve years. He assured me that to the best of his belief he was not regarded as a mental case.

Since then he has been married for twenty-five years, had two children, but been divorced. During that period he took up with a female partner. When his wife received him back into his home, this female harassed him so persistently that he finally killed her in a rage.

A plea of strong provocation was accepted. He was convicted of manslaughter and released after five years.

I am not quite sure of the dates here, but at the time of his recent crime he had been a trusted security officer for seventeen years. He worked nights, which he considered to be partly responsible for the alienation between himself and his female partner. They both came to suspect each other of infidelity. Once again he flew into a rage and strangled her, although – as mentioned earlier – it is accepted that he did not intend to kill her.

I asked him about his appearance before the Parole Board. He told me that he was only before them for twenty minutes and that the reports which they would have received about him were excellent. I was left liking him very much, but with a feeling that there was some mystery here which I had not yet penetrated. He has promised to send me his solicitor's name and address. I shall start from there.

Wednesday August 28, 1996

Visited Billy Crittenden again at Canterbury. He was his usual buoyant self. I told him that I understood a little better how he had come to be considered so troublesome in prison. His father had told me that he shouted at the jury at his trial telling them that he knew that they were going to convict him.

The accusation against him at Canterbury is that he shouts 'murderer' across the yard at another prisoner whom his evidence helped to convict of murder. He cannot persuade me now that his tone was as jocular as he likes to think.

I was interested to know what Billy thought of the rapist who was recently allowed to cross-examine his victims for six days in court. He did not answer the question directly, but told me that the young rapist who later firebombed his victim was now in Canterbury Prison. His account of the lady's character is not suitable for publication without, at least, careful research. Billy, however, admitted that firebombing, whatever your grievance, was out of order. He used the same words later in another connection, so I am beginning to assume that it is currently used by prisoners who do not wish to condemn their colleagues, but admit that they have gone a bit too far.

Friday August 30, 1996

Visited Eric Jasper in Blantyre House. He was, naturally, indignant at the way Howard had stopped the further release of prisoners several months early. Over 500 had already been released and another 400 were on the point of leaving prison when the Home Secretary stepped in.

By the time I saw Eric Jasper, Michael Howard had gained a judgment from the High Court to support his stand against a new interpretation of the 1967 Act. It is impossible to summarise the issue here, except to say that the new interpretation had been arrived at after an inquiry lasting more than six months and on the advice of Home Office lawyers.

It is not surprising that Michael Howard, as I learnt on Friday, has a new nickname in the prisons – the 'Teflon Kid'. To my shame I had never heard of Teflon, but I gather that it is used for lining saucepans because nothing sticks to it. The issue does not concern Eric immediately, but might at the end of his eight-year sentence.

Saturday August 31, 1996

Better news from Roy. He rang this morning utterly disconsolate. It is very hard to argue with a person who says that he is a hopeless character.

Soon afterwards he rang in a very different state of mind. His article, 'Why I Am a Thief', which I have been promoting with various journalist friends, has at last appeared in the *New Statesman*. I feel that this could be of untold value in getting benevolent persons interested in him; though at the age of fifty he is not likely to make a living as a journalist.

At last he saw an employment officer provided by Camden Council who gave him an hour's interview. He was apparently quite kind but left Roy with the impression – which he was quick to form – that he was unemployable. He has, however, been offered one or two courses. I am giving him lunch on Monday and shall do all in my power to persuade him to embark on one.

Monday September 2, 1996

I gave lunch to Roy whose prospects, I am afraid, remain as insecure as possible. I shall go on repeating to him, however, what I know is true, that his article in the *New Statesman* is the best thing that he has ever done. I have told him that I would explore the possibilities of his giving one or more lectures, but not until he has, on his side, explored the possibilities of various courses which have been offered him.

At the end of the week he rang up in much distress, as disconsolate as I have ever known him, to say that he was being hounded by creditors. When he carried out his big fraud on the DSS he appeared to use the credit cards of certain named individuals who are now coming after him to get their money back. Vain hope indeed.

(On Saturday I was very worried when I found him talking of leaving the country. His spirits have a way, however, of returning. So may it be this time.)

Wednesday September 4, 1996

I gave lunch to a lady called Eve Masterman, aged thirty-nine, whose husband, aged fifty, is in Brixton Prison awaiting extradition to America. I gave lunch to Eve at the request of my old friend Andrew McCooey who is roughly half my age and twice as energetic as I am now. He thinks nothing of flying to Oregon from Sittingbourne where he conducts a one-man solicitor's business.

I am visiting Ray Masterman in Brixton next Tuesday. Whether I can provide any service other than some vague encouragement remains to be seen. He skipped bail in America and was later sentenced to fifteen years in prison for illegal behaviour (I am not sure of the precise charge) towards a girl of eight. Hearing of the fifteen years I assumed that she must have been penetrated, but this was not so. She remained a virgin.

On the other hand, the children of three other neighbours testified that he had misbehaved in his dealings with them. I should have mentioned that he is a paramedic and was called in to see the child professionally. She had a rash on her bottom and other parts of her body which he treated. He felt bound to tell her mother, however, that her dirty condition must be held to be at least partly responsible for the skin disease.

My first reaction was, naturally, to assume that the mother got her own back by securing the conviction of this Englishman, resident with his wife and family in America.

It is rather harder to explain away the evidence of the other children. His wife told me that children liked coming to him and that he used to tickle them in the same way he tickled his own children. I have what I suppose can be called an open mind. It seems almost certain that he will be extradited and serve a long sentence in America.

Friday September 6, 1996

I repaired to Whitemoor. I told Eddie Richardson that, not for the first time, I had spoken to the ombudsman two days before on the telephone about his case. He could write to the ombudsman quoting me, and say that he understood that the ombudsman was 'keenly interested'. I am sure that the ombudsman will take that in good part. Until now he has obviously not been able to obtain a satisfactory explanation for why Eddie, after seven years' good conduct in prison, is still kept in a high-risk category.

As far as he could make out, two of the main factors in the decision were (1) the very large scale of Eddie's importation of drugs, and (2) Eddie's criminal connections, including, if I understood him correctly, his family connections.

I told the ombudsman to tell the 'authorities' what they may not know – that Eddie and his brother, Charlie Richardson, the one-time south London gang leader, have for some time not been on speaking terms. I still can't make out where the real animus against him lies. Left to myself I would publicise his case, but he does not wish that, at least for the moment.

Tuesday September 10, 1996

Visited Ray Masterman in Brixton Prison at the request of Andrew McCooey. I was concerned to find out from him how far he had gone in his friendly handling of the children who came to him, I gather, for his paramedical care. His wife had told me that he tickled them in exactly the same way as he tickled his own children.

I asked him pointedly where he had tickled them. He replied, without hesitation, 'Under the armpits.' He insists that part of his trouble arises from a case he was bringing against the state of Pennsylvania for compensation, a complicated matter I must look into.

I should say at once that I found him likeable and straightforward, but I have come to realise that human frailty takes strange forms. I promised him to attend the Magistrates' Court where his case will be heard on Friday.

Friday September 13, 1996

Attended Bow Street Magistrates' Court, as promised, with Ray Masterman. I had the opportunity of quite a long talk with his existing counsel, and also with the counsel who would be taking over the case when Andrew McCooey becomes his solicitor after the hearing. It was explained to me that the fact that the child remained a virgin is not an absolute defence against the charge of rape. Apparently some of his semen was found on tissues which he had used to wipe her infected bottom.

The counsel, no doubt correctly, did not contest the magistrate's order for extradition, but it is likely that there is going to be an appeal. I have spoken to Andrew since and he seems hopeful that at least a battle can be waged on Ray's behalf.

I should add that Ray's counsel, at my request, asked the magistrate for permission for me to see him and at least shake hands with him afterwards. This, the magistrate said, was outside his province. I repaired, therefore, to the office of the Securicor company responsible for holding prisoners at the court.

The young woman in charge was very strict and refused

point blank to allow me to see the prisoner because it was 'against company rules'. I became, I am afraid, rather offensive at that point. She gave me the telephone number of their regional office. When I rang up, the manager was very understanding. The young lady was quite right according to company rules, but he was sorry that I had not asked her to ring him: 'I am sure that we could have reached a compromise.' I promised to do that next time. He then offered an apology, which I thought was very decent of him.

Tuesday October 15, 1996

I can't help mentioning what follows. I attended a dinner commemorating the maiden speech of F.E. Smith, the Lord Chancellor and the first Lord Birkenhead, ninety years earlier. His elder son Freddie, later my best man, took me over to Charlton, their home, weekend after weekend, where I played tennis and golf and rowed with the 'Birker' as some of us called him.

I was the only person present who had known him at all well, and told some F.E. stories which were very successful through no skill of mine. Afterwards a legal-looking gentleman came across the room to congratulate me. I thanked him and could not help asking him what his name was. He replied, 'Michael Howard.'

Having called him the prince of darkness so often, I reacted instinctively to my own nickname for him. I quickly crossed myself. He appeared not to notice.

We chatted amicably and I was left wondering what had impelled him to approach me. Fun and games I concluded was the real answer. I have read that when at Llanelli Grammar School all the other boys were Labour and he was Conservative. Rugger was part of the religion of the school, but he played soccer.

Friday October 18, 1996

Repaired to Wormwood Scrubs where I saw Brian Vale and Uday Narayan once more. Brian Vale does not expect me to do anything to help him at the moment, but he enjoys, as I do, our conversation – he, as a member of the Socialist party of Great Britain; I, old Labour now supporting New Labour. He is, as I told him, unduly censorious about all politicians, particularly because of their refusal to come clean when found out and the refusal of their leaders to sack them.

I offered him a new thought, that all of us back up our friends and colleagues out of loyalty. The party system today undoubtedly carries this to excess. At the moment there is understandably a national desire to clean up politics, but when promoted by journalists whose own lives are on the whole probably less than healthy, it does not carry total conviction.

Uday Narayan was grateful to me for helping him, it may be, to get his appeal postponed. But his situation raises a question of principle which left me rather at a loss. He seems unable to pay a solicitor, let alone a counsel. I was under the impression that any prisoner could somehow or other obtain a solicitor. Had Uday made it impossible by rejecting those available? He denied this totally and hoped that the Citizens' Advice Bureau would help him find one. I hope so too.

Monday October 21, 1996

Visited Frederick Linale, archbishop in the Old Catholic Church, and Ray Masterman at Brixton. Frederick Linale is serving ten years for two offences against a young man, including one case of attempted buggery. Heartfelt tributes were paid to him at his trial for his services to those in greatest trouble.

Whether he erred through an excess of affection I do not wish to say. No one can question the strength of his religious belief. It seems incredible that he can have been given a ten-year prison sentence. I leave the appeal in the hands of his lawyers, but meanwhile we have had stimulating disagreements about women priests (I in favour, he against) and forgiveness. I have sent him my little book on the latter subject.

I am glad that his exceptional knowledge of languages is being used. He is acting as interpreter for South American immigrants, for example. The governor of the prison, an ex-Catholic priest I understand, is taking a keen interest in his future.

At Brixton there is no rule 43. In other words, sex offenders are in considerable danger from fellow inmates. The sooner he can be transferred the better.

Friday October 25, 1996

I visited Eddie Richardson and Des Nilsen in Whitemoor. I congratulated Eddie on his painting in this year's Koestler exhibition, in which he has won an award year after year. He did not disclose, however, what lay behind the symbolism of a fox peeping out of a kennel. Howard, no doubt, is the fox. But who or what is the kennel?

Tuesday October 29, 1996

I attended a funeral which aroused many memories – that of John Phillips, as I came to know him, the former John Vassall still referred to since his conviction in 1962 as a Russian spy.

I was pleasantly surprised by the good turnout at his funeral, particularly by those with whom he had been working in recent years. I was also glad that the press were not there to cross-examine me about my knowledge of him. They soon made up for it, however. The *Evening Standard* made him a front-page story. The *Telegraph* and *The Guardian* gave him a lot of attention. If I got as long an obituary in the *Telegraph* I should be satisfied.

John was homosexually inclined when serving as an Admiralty clerk in the British embassy in Moscow. He was blackmailed by the Russians into passing secrets to them and was eventually sentenced to many years in prison.

I got to know and like him when he was in Maidstone Prison. Later, as chairman of Sidgwick & Jackson, I was responsible for publishing his memoir. A remarkable feature of the funeral service was that it was in Latin 'at John's special request'. I was asked by more than one newspaper when John became a Catholic. That I couldn't remember, but he was a devout Catholic all the time I knew him.

Wednesday October 30, 1996

Visited once more Archbishop Frederick Linale and Ray Masterman at Brixton. Father Linale, as he is usually called in the prison, is a man of exceptional ability. (I have said the same in my time of Ian Brady, but Ian never acquired six languages. Father Linale interprets in that number of languages.)

He has grave medical problems and should have operations for a hernia and, I think, prostate trouble. These cannot be provided, he has been told, while he remains in Brixton, but it seems impossible for the moment to find him an alternative prison. I feel slightly guilty at not having been more useful to him in this respect, although I did make one telephone call to the sympathetic governor. As soon as I have finished dictating this diary, I shall write to him urgently.

Linale's property is stranded in Pentonville it seems. As I

tell prisoners often, the system is not malicious, just very incompetent. Not much consolation to them. As soon as I have finished writing to the governor of Brixton I shall write to the governor of Pentonville about Father Linale's property.

I still marvel at his persistence to break away from the Roman Catholic Church, but he is glad that his orders are still considered to be valid. He is a stickler for ritual. He finds himself unable to say Mass without the wine.

Ray Masterman can hardly be more different. His chances of remaining in Britain while his case comes to appeal in America depend on Michael Howard being persuaded that his initial trial there was profoundly unsatisfactory. A few weeks ago I would not have ventured to write to Michael Howard whom I have so often called the prince of darkness. But his approach to me at the F.E. Smith dinner makes it possible.

On the other hand Ray's case is so complicated that one cannot expect Michael Howard to give much time to it. I told Ray that I had it in mind to write to him when the time came and have it looked into by his officials.

Friday November 1, 1996

Visits to Andrew Gorgio at the Scrubs in the morning and to Tony Wolf at Pentonville in the afternoon. Andrew Gorgio is the friend of William Close, and was convicted along with William of the murder of a man with a criminal past who was beating up William's mother. I had a long and pleasant talk with William in Brixton some time ago, but when I visited Gartree recently, where he now resides, he did not wish to see me for reasons unknown.

Gorgio told me the same story as William. On the face of it, it was extraordinary that they were convicted of murder, although I suppose that, in William's case, the jury concentrated on what seemed a likely motive. I doubt if there is much that I can do to help Gorgio, though I feel confident that he and William are innocent. The evidence against them seems almost non-existent. They were not picked out, for example, in an identity parade.

All I can do is to make contact with his solicitor, a lady in whom he has much confidence. So far he has been told that there are no grounds for an appeal.

In the afternoon went to Pentonville. Ten minutes were wasted in a ridiculous fashion while I was trying to enter this prison which I have visited so often and where I had an appointment to see Tony Wolf. I was asked to prove my identity, which produced a ludicrous argument in which I may or may not have appeared to advantage.

I should explain that new rules have been introduced at Pentonville since September. One is now expected to produce an official document, such as a driving licence, a passport or a birth certificate. I produced my travel permit which includes a photo card by London Transport and read as follows: 'Holder: Earl Longford. For concessionary travel permit. For conditions see over.'

This was not good enough for the young official. A senior prison officer had to be called, and later a duty governor. In the end they allowed themselves to be convinced by a letter from the aforementioned Gorgio. It is almost unbelievable!

Luckily I was able to wrongfoot them. I told them, which they more or less had to believe, that when I booked the legal visit I was not informed about the new identity requirement. I extracted a grudging apology, but I shall write to the governor of Pentonville about this also.

Tony Wolf, on the face of it, is a sad figure though he does not seem unduly depressed. He told me this time that he had been sexually abused from four to fifteen and obviously felt that this had helped to make him a congenital thief or fraudsman.

Friday November 22, 1996

To Pentonville. I had arranged to see a prisoner called Tony Wolf, but of course I did not spell it out on the telephone. When I arrived there was a Tony *Woolfe* to meet me. I became very annoyed with what seemed to me a typical example of prison inefficiency. But, on reflection, I realised that they were not to blame.

When I got back to the House of Lords I found a letter from the real Tony Wolf, saying that he had been moved to Wormwood Scrubs.

Tony Woolfe at Pentonville told me a sad story, though not one which seemed to have destroyed him. Aged thirty-three he has been in prison for twelve years out of his adult life, as a result of an addiction to drink and drugs which has led him to commit many thefts and burglaries. He told me that he had learnt to take drugs at thirteen and was in trouble of some kind even earlier. The old, old story – his mother had left home and there was no one to look after him.

He is now receiving intensive counselling and would love to get rid of his tragic addictions. His greatest desire is to get to a drug-free prison such as Downview in Surrey. I have promised to write to the governor to see whether this can be managed.

Wednesday November 27, 1996

Visited the real Tony Wolf in Wormwood Scrubs. Now there is a real unfortunate for you. He looks buoyant enough, but his story is one of almost unrelieved awfulness. As a boy he was sexually abused by his mother's partner and the partner's friends. 'Where was your father?' I asked. 'I was born as a result of rape,' he told me. He has been in and out of prison for stealing or fraud until reaching his present age of late twenties. He was sent to a therapeutic institution by the court.

He is now, he tells me, HIV-positive as a result of being buggered by two prisoners in Leyhill Prison.

I have since spoken to his solicitor, who has tried to help him for years. Tony has been seen by a number of psychiatrists, but none of them seem ready to describe him as mentally ill. As Tony says himself, he faces quite a severe prison sentence.

Wednesday December 11, 1996

Interesting visit to Wandsworth seeing Father Linale with his protégé Paul Orriss. Father Linale had asked me to take an interest in this young man.

Paul Orriss told me that he had been raped by a cell-mate in Durham Prison. He is quite a large young man, and I could not help wondering whether it was a completed act or an attempt. He reported the rape, but was threatened by other inmates that if he persisted with the charge, he would have his cheeks cut about.

He therefore dropped it, but got the worst of all worlds. He was regarded as a 'grass' and, for his own safety, removed from Durham, his home town, to Wandsworth. He now asks me to persuade the authorities to transfer him back to Durham.

He has eleven months of his sentence to serve (four years for robbery – two years, eight months, in practice). His mother is dying of cancer and is given four months to live.

I pointed out to him that the authorities might reply that he had left Durham for his own protection. Was it safe for him to return? His reply to that is that he would be ready to go on rule 43 or the equivalent and hence be segregated. I have, accordingly, written to the governor of Wandsworth pleading for his transfer. I still can never discover who really decides on these transfers. It seems, however, a good idea to start with the governor of Wandsworth. I would not like to seem to bypass him.

Finally, I saw Tony Wolf at Wormwood Scrubs who expects a custodial sentence on Tuesday. He is convinced that he will never recover from his addiction to stealing until he is given prolonged therapy. He is very doubtful, as I am, whether this is available in prison. He feels sure that he would be able to obtain it outside.

In the meantime Grendon Underwood in Buckinghamshire seems his best chance. He will make contact with me as soon as the result of his court appearance on Tuesday is known. On this occasion he did not mention the fact that he has AIDS. I am afraid that I forgot to ask him.

Monday December 30, 1996

At Bullingdon in Oxfordshire I found Charlie Bronson as buoyant as ever and better situated than he was in Wakefield where he was 'in a cage' – that is, behind bars. He tells me that there is a BBC *Panorama* programme coming out about him in February. At any rate, a programme of some kind.

He is now quite sure that he would much prefer to be in Broadmoor. A psychiatrist from Broadmoor has visited him and agreed, it appears, that that is the right place for him. There seem, however, to be various difficulties in the way. I shall be pursuing the matter afresh with his solicitor. He tells me also that he has completed a joint book with a lady in America who is coming to England this summer. It sounds unlikely, but Charlie springs surprises.

Friday January 3, 1997

Visited Tony Wolf, Uday Narayan and Brian Vale in the Scrubs. Tony's problems on paper are appalling and yet he remains cheerful. The current question is how he can be given treatment, before his release in September, that will prevent him going straight back into crime. I have promised to arrange for a visitor from the New Bridge, but have since discovered that he must write to them and make the request himself. I am sure that a prison visitor could be very helpful to him, but it must be one with plenty of time to give him.

I did not realise that he became a Mormon last February, but is in touch with the Catholic chaplain whom I have promised to speak to about him. He told me that, though never married and only twenty-eight, he has had two children by two different partners. The first was killed in a car accident, the second murdered by being thrown against a wall by his former partner's new partner. The last named is doing a life sentence for murder. Tony says that he cannot forgive him, but feels sorry for him and would like to see him released.

Brian Vale is one of the few prisoners who appears to be happy in prison. He has just heard that he has passed the first stage of his Open University degree and is full of intellectual activity. He is equally contemptuous of capitalism and communism and does not think highly of the co-operative movement. I tell him that his socialist dream seems to impute a degree of wisdom to the masses which, in my assessment of human nature, is unreal.

I got through to him, I think, when I told him of my experience at New Horizon, the youth centre I founded in 1968. After I ceased to be chairman the organisation was determined to try a collective experience which, as I expected, did not endure. Brian Vale agreed that government by committee is not satisfactory. We shall continue the discussion next time.

Wednesday January 15, 1997

To Brixton where Ray Masterman is convinced that my visits have led to a certain amount of discrimination against him in the prison. Nevertheless he wants me to continue to come and see him.

I am about to sit down and write to the governor asking whether it is humane to keep anyone in his cell for twenty-three hours a day. The governor, a former Catholic priest, is, I like to think, well-disposed towards me. I have not met him, but I wrote a very favourable review of his prison book.

Ray would really like a transfer to a prison nearer his family, but the first move is to be the letter to the governor. I am not sure, from what he tells me, that Ray is always as subordinate to the prison staff as discretion would suggest.

Friday January 17, 1997

Visited David Rundle after quite an interval in Littlehey Prison. It is now several years since David was recalled to prison, in which time he has never been allowed to appear before a tribunal. Nor has any real reason been given in my eyes for his recall.

He has now been promised a move at the end of January to Leyhill Open Prison in Gloucestershire, but he would very much rather go to Ford at Arundel in Sussex where he was at the end of his sentence. It would be very much easier for his children to visit him. His mother alas! does not seem well enough to visit him.

I have promised to write to Ann Widdecombe, the

Minister for Prisons, though am anxious not to raise false hopes. In the report of his prison probation officer David is said to have made substantial progress in understanding his troubles with women, but he needs further offender-related treatment at Leyhill. The probation officer whose say-so originally brought David back to prison now firmly supports his release. So the struggle goes on.

Wednesday January 22, 1997

10–11.30 a.m. Wormwood Scrubs. Tony Wolf as full of problems as always. He looks quite cheerful. His latest role is to act as a prosecution witness in a murder trial. Two prisoners, now in the same wing as him in the Scrubs, are being charged with murder; one of them confessed to Tony, and Tony is now giving evidence for the prosecution. He assumes, not unreasonably, that when the news reaches his fellow prisoners he will be in grave danger.

After Tony, saw Brian Vale, always a stimulating intellectual challenge. He is now studying sociology and asked me what I thought of postmodernism. I had never heard of it. He had only just heard of it, but would tell me more about it next time.

3 p.m. Visited my new friend, as I am happy to call him, Archbishop Linale – Father Fred, as he seems to be known to most of his flock. He seems to feel that in a physical sense I am being helpful to him. He is in a warm cell and at last seems to be receiving proper medical attention.

The question, however, of his human rights and his ability, therefore, to say Mass remains unresolved. The representative of the Catholic archbishop of Southwark says that is not their responsibility. I am trying, therefore, to reach the chief Catholic prison chaplain, but he is away for ten days.

Thursday January 23, 1997

A busy day. Five radio programmes about Myra. The *Daily Mail* had come out with a disgraceful front page devoted entirely to Myra and the news, not yet confirmed, that Howard will decide that she should stay in prison until she dies. As always they were unable to find any rational person to defend that position.

Oxford Radio, in the end, produced a woman who said that hanging was too good for Myra, but went on to say that matters should be taken out of the hands of the politicians and left to the judiciary which, of course, is what Myra's lawyers are now demanding. I am not proud of my replies to her and her like. I suggested that she was sick and needed a lot of help. Peter Timms, the former governor of Maidstone Prison and a friend of Myra, seems to have done better on television in demanding that she should be treated like anyone else.

Thursday January 30, 1997

Jack Straw, Shadow Home Secretary, addressed the Labour peers. The audience was courteous but I would think sceptical. I put a question in this way: 'When I visit prisons, as I do once or twice a week, I am always asked by staff and prisoners, "Will things be any better under Labour?" May I have an answer from Jack, with whom we all sympathise in his tragic dilemma?'

I was referring of course to the clash between traditional Labour support for penal reform and a desperate competition for votes with the Conservatives. Of course we are all longing to win the election. Jack talked away in reply, but he reminded me of the Irish orator who wound up a speech by saying, 'Mind you, I've said nothing.'

Jack Straw is recognised by all of us as a decent man with

plenty of ability and is, I believe, a Christian socialist. I did not really expect a reply to my question, but I told him it was the least unpleasant one I would ask him.

Later I was back in the champagne culture, and though it was an evening affair, and I like to go to bed early, I was much more in my element. I was proposing the health of my oldest friend, Maureen Dufferin, widow of my Oxford colleague Basil, the Marquess of Dufferin and Ava, on her ninetieth birthday and was rightly introduced as having been best man at her wedding sixty-seven years ago.

I produced some excellent anecdotes from the good old days and wound up by saying that then, as always, she had personality. No one ever had more. This was once written of W.B. Yeats, but it was generally felt appropriate to Maureen as she sat there with a duke on her right hand and the Queen Mother beyond.

As far as I could see she was the only person who didn't touch a drop of alcohol. Elizabeth and I danced once round the room. I then dragged her away. Left to herself she would have stayed there all night. The Queen Mother danced with our son Thomas, which for a lady of ninety-six was very impressive.

Sunday February 9, 1997

The main event for me this week was the news that Michael Howard had confirmed the ruling that Myra will never come out of prison. I was on five programmes subsequently, including the *Six O'Clock News*, *Newsnight* and Radio 4.

Wednesday February 12, 1997

With great difficulty arranged a legal visit to Maria Pearson at Holloway for 9 a.m. When I got there I was told through the ghastly glass wall that my visit had been refused. I pointed out that the governor's secretary had told me yesterday that it was confirmed. I was told it was refused this morning.

I asked to see the governor's secretary, but was requested to move on as I was holding up the queue. Eventually I was told that someone would come down to see me. Next thing I was told that the visit was now accepted. So, I made my way up to the place for legal visits. Maria met me and told me that she had understood that the visit was for ten o'clock. She has been convicted of murder, but an appeal is planned on mental grounds.

I should mention here that my relations with prison staff are generally good except when conducted through a glass wall on arrival. Occasionally, but not often, there is a little slot in the wall through which it is easier to converse.

Thursday February 13, 1997

A fine day in the history of the House of Lords. A crucial amendment to Michael Howard's new Criminal Justice Bill was carried by 180 to 172 votes. The judges were solidly against him. The attack was led by Lord Carlisle – a former Home Office minister, a former chairman of the Parole Board, and now a recorder. The particular amendment carried gave back a substantial measure of discretion to the judges of which the bill would have deprived them. Michael Howard has sworn to reverse the decision in the Commons. With any luck the arguments over the bill will lead to it being overtaken by the general election.

Friday February 14, 1997

Another visit to Whitemoor to see Eddie and Des. The usual delay on entry. I discovered, at last, that my visits are always treated as social visits, not legal, which they are in other prisons. This means waiting twenty minutes instead of going in straight away. I hope to rectify this next time.

Des seemed fairly happy. He was much cheered to hear from Gordon Honeycombe, the former newscaster who is editing his manuscript, that he is full of admiration. I expect to see Honeycombe shortly.

Tuesday February 18, 1997

An unusual visit. I was taken down by car to support my new friend Bob Tierney in the launch of his book of memoirs. I have described it in my introduction as a remarkable book by a remarkable man which is certainly no overstatement.

Bob spent seventeen years off and on in prison, was a drug addict and alcoholic, but is now on the point of becoming a probation officer, a unique life story in my experience. John McVicar, a prisoner convicted of grave crimes and now a writer on prisons, is one possible comparison. Peter Thompson, four years in Broadmoor and the creator and inspirer of the Matthew Trust, is another.

The Probation Service was giving a party and the Mayor of Reading was present. Bob is happily married to a charming lady whom I met at the party. They have five children. Bob revealed an extraordinary capacity for comic entertainment in his speech which should stand him in good stead in whatever lies ahead for him.

I was taken down by someone almost equally remarkable. Many years ago he was Bob's partner in crime and later he seems to have gone deeper and deeper into it. But at a certain point he found the Lord and is now in charge of a Pentecostal church. His wife was a Salvation Army social worker when she met him, but is now his full-time assistant.

Wednesday February 19, 1997

Another visit to my now very good friend the archbishop, in Wandsworth, whose medical needs are finally being properly attended to, though he is still awaiting the necessary operation for his hernia. I have failed rather badly to make any progress with the Catholic authorities regarding permission for him to say Mass, but at least he is being visited by a priest of his own offshoot of Catholicism and also by the local Roman Catholic priest who became his friend in Brixton.

Thursday February 20, 1997

The committee stage in the Lords of the Criminal Justice Bill. The government was not defeated again, although there was plenty of criticism, amendments moved but withdrawn for discussion later. On one amendment, moved by the Liberals, I differed from the party leadership to the extent of voting for it when they abstained. But so did two other senior Labour peers. So no eyebrows were raised.

I moved an amendment of my own which I withdrew to enable the House to consider it more carefully. It would have placed mandatory life prisoners (in other words, murderers) on the same footing as so-called discretionary life prisoners. This mirrors the case of my friend David Rundle, who was recalled to prison on the say-so of a probation officer.

Friday February 21, 1997

Visited a new prisoner in Nottingham Prison at the urgent request of his wife. She was a psychiatric social worker, now suffering from multiple sclerosis, who originally formed a pen friendship with him and then married him. They are evidently very much in love.

He is a new type of murderer to me. Indeed I don't like to use the word about him, but it is a fact that he pleaded guilty to murder. His first wife hanged herself. He had a mental breakdown. He became infatuated with a new woman. He and she hired a hit man to murder her husband. All three got life sentences. He was given a tariff of twelve years which was raised to fourteen by the Lord Chief Justice.

His psychiatric condition, when he was responsible for his share of the crime, was apparently not placed before the judge. He is a gentle humorous man and I will do all I can to help him, though whether that amounts to anything remains very much to be seen.

After some hesitation I reminded him that Myra Hindley, a nice young Catholic woman, had become infatuated with Ian Brady, her young boss, very gifted but very crazy, and became his accomplice in terrible murders. I think that he was grateful for the comparison.

I was left with a more general question when I came away. He is attending some psychology course which seems to be helping him to recover a little of his self-esteem, which has been largely destroyed by the tragedy. How lifelong remorse can be combined with the aforesaid self-esteem is something I will go on thinking about.

Wednesday February 26, 1997

Brian Vale, as always, provokes a stimulating discussion. He is well into his Open University degree course by now, concentrating on the Enlightenment, but Marx remains his deity. I suggested to him that Marx would interpret Blair's success quite easily. Up to now Labour has appealed to the self-interest of the working classes and the idealism of the middle classes. Now they're appealing to the self-interest of the middle classes and until they lose the support of the working classes they have the majority of the country on their side. He seems to agree with me that that is how Marx would view the situation.

The next day the staff at Wormwood Scrubs went on strike, but came off it after a few hours. They were complaining, apparently, about the new distribution of shifts. My complaint on Friday would have been about the delays in admitting legal visitors. I arrived at ten o'clock. We all went in quite soon afterwards, but two solicitors had been waiting half an hour. No one ever knows whose fault it is.

Incidentally, one of the solicitors told me that his partner worked with a barrister friend of mine. I said I assumed that his 'partner' was a woman. He replied, 'No, a man.'

We had time for a brief discussion on homosexuality. I told him that from his point of view my record was a mixed one. I had opened in 1957 a debate in favour of the Wolfenden Report in the Lords before any other public man would touch it (it would have permitted sex between males over twenty-one in private). Since then, however, I have been strongly against any reduction of the permitted age, being all too well aware of the corruption of rent boys by middle-aged gentlemen.

Incidentally, when the Wolfenden principle was at last being put into a bill, Field-Marshall Lord Montgomery had moved an amendment to confine adult sex to men over eighty. Speaking as an octogenarian, he assured the House of Lords that there was no danger after that age.

Wednesday March 5, 1997

Another very enjoyable visit to my new and now-admired friend Archbishop Linale, or Father Fred, as I am learning to call him.

The news on his front is a good deal better. The Anglican

chaplain in Wandsworth has come out very strongly on his side. I gather that it will now be possible for a priest of Father Fred's small communion to come to hear his confession.

All that remains is the need to obtain a thimbleful of wine to enable him to say Mass in his cell. The Catholic chaplain, aged about twenty-eight, came to see Father Fred white-faced to say that I have been complaining to him, and more significantly perhaps the chaplain had been rebuked on the same subject by a high official in the Home Office.

I still don't know how the Home Office got wind of this, but it is all to the good. The next move seems to lie with me and probably involves an approach to Ann Widdecombe, Minister for Prisons and a recent Catholic convert. It seems that when she became a Catholic, Father Fred, then at liberty, wrote to her and received a warm reply.

Meanwhile he has been denounced at some length in the *News of the World* in what sounds like a defamatory fashion. It seems that the article contains serious misstatements. An action for libel is presumably beyond the means of Father Fred. It looks as if a complaint should be made to the Press Complaints Commission. It happens, however, that I was recently given lunch by the present editor of the *News of the World*, so perhaps something can be done there.

Friday March 7, 1997

Visited Tony Wolf. At one time I thought that he was suffering from AIDS, but no mention was made of it on this occasion. He expects to come out of prison in September and go to live with his mother.

I am glad that someone from the New Bridge is coming to visit him shortly. His future must be regarded as very uncertain, but he is highly intelligent – although one of the staff said 'very cunning', if his financial operations are any guide. He is genuinely determined to turn over a new leaf and I remain hopeful he can pull it off.

I also visited Robert Brand, a client of Andrew McCooey, who had asked me to see him. He was small and shy. I think that he was a little bewildered by my visit, but on the whole seemed to welcome it.

He was serving a sentence of four years for robbery, never having been in prison before, when a young man was put in the cell along with him. Robert Brand battered the unfortunate youth while he was asleep and might well have killed him. It seems decided that he should go to Broadmoor which would certainly seem to be the right place for him.

I asked him the usual unanswerable question: why did you do it? He referred to voices, which is usually a sign of schizophrenia. It is no surprise that after being seen by a psychiatrist he is bound for Broadmoor.

Wednesday March 12, 1997

Another interesting visit to Father Fred. I have written making formal application to Ann Widdecombe, Minister for Prisons, to allow him the thimbleful of wine he needs to say Mass.

Here there are wheels within wheels which should work out well for Father Fred. Ann Widdecombe is not only a Catholic convert, as previously mentioned, but was instructed prior to her conversion by my friend Father Michael Seed (she is one of his famous 'seedlings'). By a lucky chance I gave Michael Seed lunch on Tuesday. He has not met Father Fred, but knows quite a lot about the problems involved, having been approached by the police when Father Fred was first arrested. He is on the right side of the argument and with his permission I have suggested in my letter that Ann should consult him.

I have rung up Phil Hall, editor of the *News of the World*

about their article which described Father Fred's church as the most evil one on earth. I asked him what he proposed to do to put the matter right. The article contained flagrant misstatements. It described a certain gentleman called Simmons, who has been in prison more than once, as the leader of the church in Father Fred's absence. This is totally untrue. I asked Hall, for example, whether he would accept a letter from me putting the matter straight. It would no doubt be a highly critical letter. He told me that the author of the article is abroad, but he would give me an answer by this Friday.

Friday March 14, 1997

Visited the Courts of Justice in the hope of hearing the case in which Roisin McAliskey is pleading for bail. She is the daughter of Bernadette Devlin whom I welcomed in 1969 to Parliament when she had won a by-election in Northern Ireland. Listening in the gallery I heard this 21-year-old girl make what Norman St John Stevas has since called the most brilliant maiden speech since that of F.E. Smith in 1906.

Out of admiration for her mother I visited Roisin some weeks ago in prison, and went to the High Court out of some kind of Irish feeling of solidarity. In fact the case was heard in chambers, but I spent a profitable hour and three quarters acquiring knowledge outside the court. I was also able to wave my Irish rugby union tie at the photographers and the small Irish crowd waiting outside.

Her bail, regrettably, was refused. I expect to visit her on Wednesday.

Wednesday March 19, 1997

Visited Roisin McAliskey for the second time, and Maria Pearson in Holloway.

Roisin has become something of an international figure since I last saw her. At any rate the Irish Foreign Secretary and other international leaders were taking an active interest in her position.

There is not much I can do to help Roisin, though she is a sweet, small person. She is in the best possible legal hands. She surprised me by saying that when liberated she wants to go to Germany to establish her innocence for all time. I can't help hoping that she reconsiders her decision when the time comes.

Maria Pearson's case for a new reference to the Appeal Court is based on the argument that she was mentally disturbed when she killed the lady who threatened her marriage. Today she is full of charm and potential intelligence, but she says herself that she is far from well and would benefit, I am sure, from medical care.

Friday March 28, 1997

Visited an old friend of seventeen years, David Rundle. He is now back at Ford Prison in Arundel where he served the last part of his sentence before his subsequent recall. Leaving the house at ten past nine to walk to Etchingham station, I travelled in eight trains there and back before reaching home at 6.30 p.m.

David finds life much better at Ford. He has the same case officer as before, whom he likes very much. He seems uncertain about his probation officer, but did not wish me to intervene. The probation officer in prison is all-important to the recall prisoner. David got on badly with his at Littlehey.

He asked me how he should reply to the probation officer when asked about his unfortunate relationship with women – a murdered wife, a mistress who turned against him and a lady who proved his downfall and led to his recall.

The answer he usually gives is, 'I felt sorry for them.' I told him that I felt that that was very unconvincing. It would be much better to say that he was at a loss to provide an answer. I hope for the best in his relationship with his new probation officer.

The serious defect of the present system is that far too much depends on the say-so of the probation officer inside and outside prison. In my experience the probation officer is inclined to play safe to the disadvantage of the prisoner.

Friday April 11, 1997

Another bad reception at Holloway. The very helpful governor's secretary had promised me a visiting time between 9.30 and 11.30 a.m. I told her that I expected to arrive about 10.

In fact I turned up a bit earlier. I was told by the young woman behind the thick glass wall that I could not see anybody before 10.30. The usual bad-tempered exchange followed.

Eventually I saw Roisin McAliskey soon after 10, and later made a complaint about the original muddle. Holloway, at the moment, wins the lowest marks from me for the reception arrangements. As usual one can never discover who is to blame. Certainly not the governor (who not so long ago apologised to me for the removal of my handkerchief) or his admirable secretary.

Roisin was, as usual, imperturbable. She insists that she has never been to Germany and today told me that the witness who alleged she had appears to be retracting the claim. She expects to appear in court on May 6 at Bow Street. I promised to attend, if possible.

If all goes well she should be released and able to return to Northern Ireland in time for the arrival of her baby on May 30. If she is freed she hopes to be married in County Tyrone on July 22 and has asked me to attend if possible. I would love to, but wonder if in fact I will be able to do it. She had been approached to stand as an Independent candidate for Parliament but had declined. She agreed with me that notable Irish men and women had been elected before now from prison.

Maria Pearson is a one-off. The prison authorities may heave a sigh of relief at the thought. When asked whether she was ready to receive a visit from me she replied, 'I will telephone Lord Longford on the subject.' Not surprisingly, perhaps, she is not the favourite of all the staff.

She tells me that she is far from well, which I am sure is true. I have taken up with the prison the need for medical attention. She tells me also that the copy of Derek Lewis's book which I promised her has never arrived.

To my surprise when I entered the small room reserved for my talk with Maria I found that we were not alone. A large friendly prison officer was prepared to supervise the visit. After I protested and she had made the necessary enquiries, she withdrew. I was afterwards told that she had only recently arrived in Holloway which was a pretty poor excuse. The mistake was obviously not hers.

Many years ago my visits were supervised. Once when Myra Hindley was in court after an attempted escape with a prison visitor, I gave evidence to character. The prosecuting lawyer put it to me, 'Would you say that you were under Miss Hindley's thrall, Lord Longford?'

'That may or may not be so,' I replied, 'but at least the supervising officer was there to make sure that nothing untoward took place.' It is many years, however, since a supervising officer sat in on one of my visits, though sometimes the door has been left open.

Maria is very impatient about the delay in regard to her case. Under a new arrangement it is not left to the Home

Secretary to decide whether she should be allowed to appeal. I tried to persuade her that the new Criminal Appeals Review Commission offered her better hope. She is somewhat sceptical.

Tuesday April 15, 1997

Another visit to Father Fred. His health seems to be under control, though he bears up gallantly under various ailments. He agrees with Michael Seed's suggestion that he should wait for a new government before trying to secure full permission for him to say Mass.

Wednesday April 16, 1997

Reported at Southwark Crown Court at 10 a.m. to give evidence if required for John Masterson. John, an old friend, whom I first met when he was in prison many years ago, has avoided trouble for twelve years, but has now been embroiled in a fight in the course of which he smashed a window and, it is alleged, threatened somebody with violence. It is agreed that he never hit anybody.

The other two defendants were a former Commonwealth heavyweight boxing champion and his son. There is no doubt that the father beat up somebody and told me that the man in question had then attacked his son.

I spent two hours outside the court while father and son argued as to how far they were going to plead guilty. I retired having promised to write a letter on behalf of John.

Friday April 18, 1997

Visited Eddie Richardson and Des Nilsen once again at Whitemoor. I always expect an annoying experience when I arrive at Whitemoor and I was not disappointed this time. One has to leave one's money at the visiting centre about 150 yards away, and buy tickets for tea. I, forgetfully, left £1 coins in my pocket which I duly declared on arrival, but by that time, in accordance with the Whitemoor routine, I had removed my shoes. I was told that I must take the money back to the centre, having first put on my shoes. My request to leave my money with the gate person while I visited the prisoners was refused.

The time wasted was added to by my protests which produced one of the governors, but the phrase 'rules are rules' became a kind of chant. Incidentally, at the visiting centre, the lady in charge was ready to take care of my bag in her office instead of putting it into a locker – in other words she stretched the rules in my favour.

Thinking over these little nuisances that do not only occur in prisons, I conclude that anyone acting on their own may well be reasonable, but if several people are present they all become zombies.

No special news from Eddie and Des. Eddie is waiting for two kinds of news. One, regarding his status. Two, regarding his parole. One is decided by the Home Office, the other from within the Prison Service, but they are interlinked, of course, for as long as he is high-risk category A he cannot receive parole. He does not wish me to act until after a new Minister for Prisons is appointed.

Tuesday April 22, 1997

Visited a new prisoner, the Hon. Dr Caffyd Smith. He obtained his doctorate in the history of art, and is the heir to a Welsh peerage.

He is serving a sentence for some kind of fraud in the course of his art-dealing business. He came to see me a little while ago at the House of Lords and later produced a very perceptive interview in a magazine. I was particularly glad that he quoted something that I said when he asked me if I had ever given spiritual help to a prisoner. I replied, 'No, never, but I have received spiritual help from Frederick Linale, archbishop in the Old Catholic Church, now serving a ten-year sentence for a grave sexual lapse.'

I was then under the impression that Caffyd Smith was a member of the prison education staff, but I liked him just as much when I discovered that he was a prisoner. I am looking forward to working with him at the House of Lords in the near future.

Wednesday April 23, 1997

Another visit to Maria Pearson, that strange, charming woman in Holloway. I had confirmed the visit for ten o'clock with the governor's secretary the previous day, but on arrival I was told, without explanation, that the visit had been refused.

There was the usual shouting match through the glass wall with me demanding to see the governor's secretary or duty governor. Eventually I was told that the visit had been accepted, so after half an hour's wrangling I met Maria Pearson.

It appears that she had been escorted, on my previous visit, from her wing by a prison officer. This time she had been told to go along with a crowd of prisoners and wait an hour or so for a visit. She had declined. Eventually, she got her way.

No one can pretend that she is an easy prisoner to cope with, but equally, I could have been told in the first place that they were looking into the matter. If I had been less bloody-minded, I would have gone away with my tail between my legs.

She had, as usual, a list of complaints. I am sure that more attention should be paid to her health. I can also sympathise with her impatience, to put it mildly, at the long delay in her case being heard. The new machinery taking the decision away from the Home Secretary and giving it to an independent commission sounds better on paper, but there are 300 cases on the waiting list; one can only beg her to be patient.

Friday April 25, 1997

Visited Belmarsh Prison. Hubert Carnegie, a black Jamaican, had asked to see me as a matter of urgency.

He has lived in England twenty-nine years, but I found it difficult to follow his English, though it was grammatically correct. He is doing five years for rape, and I am ready to agree with his solicitor, whom I spoke to afterwards on the telephone, that he is probably innocent.

He would not claim to come out of it with a clean sheet. He admits to picking up a lady at Victoria Station and taking her back to his flat and having sex with her. He admits giving her £20, but failed to give her another £20 which she demanded.

She dashed off to the police, covered with scratches and torn drawers, which he insists were self-inflicted.

Unfortunately, the request by his lawyers that he should be allowed to appeal was refused. It seems unlikely, therefore, that he will be allowed to obtain legal aid.

He is a pathetic lonely figure, who I understand lives with his brother when not in prison, but, having been divorced, he now has a girlfriend so there may be light at the end of his tunnel.

Wednesday April 30, 1997

Valuable talk with Governor Pearson, director of security at the Prison Service. Mr Pearson was exceptionally sympathetic and readily accepted my claim that I had visited more prisoners than any other amateur.

He was aware that in January I had been told in Parliament that the Prison Service was taking a new hard look at the arrangements for visitors. He promised to be ready with an answer if I asked a question at the beginning of June. He gave me the encouraging news that in future those receiving visiting orders would be given information as to searching and identification processes at individual prisons. I pulled out my bus pass, as on an earlier occasion, with its photograph, and hoped that such passes would be made acceptable in future.

Sunday May 4, 1997

This has been the week of the most traumatic general election in my lifetime. The comparisons, I suppose, would be with 1931 and 1945.

Penal affairs had hardly figured in the election, for which I suppose I should be thankful. No one imagines that penal reform would have been a vote winner. The truth about the political aspect of all this was expressed to me some time ago by Patricia (Baroness) Hollis, one of our most successful shadow ministers in the Lords. The phrase she used was significant: 'We've neutralised the Tories on law and order.'

Be all that as it may, I have just drafted a speech for the debates that will follow the opening of Parliament. I describe this as the most critical moment in the history of penal reform in this country. I call attention to the fact that the new Cabinet contains half a dozen Christian socialists, notably Tony Blair and Jack Straw, so I strike an optimistic note. No harm in that occasionally.

Wednesday May 7, 1997

Another visit to Maria Pearson at Holloway. I have come to expect something to complain about every time I visit Holloway, and I was not disappointed. They stamped a mark on my wrist on the way in to make sure that if a prisoner posing as me tried to escape, the prisoner would be spotted. This makes sense in men's prisons, though the practice varies, but it makes no sense at all for a man going into women's prisons.

They obviously didn't take it very seriously, because they did not bother to look at my wrist on the way out. When I told the official that I would be making a complaint in due course he retorted, 'Some of the women in here look very like men.'

Maria was in her usual sprightly form, ticking me off for this and that. She is very upset because under the new regulations the property in her cell will be reduced to two suitcases. I promised to take it up with the governor or his excellent secretary. The latter, totally blind, I understand, is exceptionally helpful.

But I can't help feeling that Maria won't win this one. More seriously, she is desperately anxious for her case to be considered.

Later Andrew McCooey persuaded me to accompany him to Swaleside Prison on the Isle of Sheppey. He promised me that I would meet a remarkable prisoner, and as usual he kept his word.

William Hennesy was convicted of murdering his aunt when he was fourteen. Twenty years later he is still in prison. There is, of course, some explanation. He has tried to escape more than once. On one occasion he spent ten months on the run. He earned his living by teaching music, but also obtained money from a hotel by false pretences, which led to his being picked up.

Now he is, I verily believe, a reformed character in the sense that, having been antisocial for many years, he has found religion and is working on behalf of, rather than against, his fellow men.

I had a long talk with the chaplain, who, along with others from the prison, had testified before a panel on William's behalf on the previous day. It seems that in February 1996, he at last became a committed Christian. He is now a chapel orderly and teaches music in the prison.

It was good to learn that the hearing before the panel on the previous day in the prison deeply impressed him. He heard his whole life rehearsed from various points of view and was deeply grateful for the way in which the prison staff had spoken up for him.

Andrew was arguing that at the very least he ought to be moved from category B to category D, in other words to an open prison with a chance of early release. But he had submitted strongly that after twenty years in prison this man, whom no one thought was dangerous, could now go free.

I kept telling him that I would do anything in my power, but he must not build false hopes on my intervention. If the moment arose that Andrew thought I could help with the new Home Secretary, I would write to him.

I was much interested in a reply to a question I put to William. Taking his life as a whole, could he have been treated differently once he was convicted (he had had a number of unfortunate experiences earlier)? He said that the worst thing that happened to him was going to prison when he was fourteen, where, in my language, he developed an antisocial attitude. Afterwards he went to an excellent children's establishment, but the damage had been done.

He is convinced that young offenders should be treated by social workers rather than by prison officers. I think that there is a great deal in what he says.

Wednesday May 14, 1997

A rather difficult visit to my friend Father Fred. He is very anxious for me to help a young man aged twenty-one who has not been long in Wandsworth. He has already undergone some painful experiences.

The Samaritans are allowed to appoint 'listeners' among the prisoners who act as what one might call para-counsellors. Unfortunately the 'listener' appointed to help Father Fred's young friend made indecent advances to him.

Complaints were made by Father Fred, among others, and the listener was withdrawn from contact with the young man, but he is still functioning as an authorised 'listener'. Father Fred wants me to urge the Samaritans to prevent him continuing as a 'listener'.

But that is far from all. A young man in the prison has stirred up trouble for the young friend of Father Fred. It is all very difficult for me to cope with, but I shall do my best.

Friday May 16, 1997

Visited Eddie Richardson and Des Nilsen once again at Whitemoor. Eddie is pleased and more grateful than I probably deserve for my help in getting him removed from high-risk category A. He is still a category A, but that should not prevent him from being transferred to Long Lartin in Worcestershire where he is anxious to make a fresh start. His record appears to have been impeccable during his eight years in prison.

Nevertheless, while in Whitemoor he has three times been removed for a month on the grounds, quite unsupported by evidence, that he stirs up trouble. He is convinced that his own wing governor is, for reasons he cannot understand, suspicious of him. At his request, I saw a duty governor who told me that this particular wing governor was aged thirty-two and expected to have a brilliant career in the service. The duty governor brought home to me what I suppose I should have realised earlier, namely that allegations of this kind are often based on information supplied by prisoners, the source of which cannot be revealed.

Tuesday May 20, 1997

Attended, as a guest, the annual conference of the Official Prison Visitors. One of the two main speakers was my old friend Bob Tierney. The other was deputy head of the Prison Service.

I told the audience that when I became an official prison visitor in Oxford sixty years ago we were forbidden to maintain contact with prisoners on their release. Many of us, in fact, disregarded the instruction.

In the evening the first really good news about Myra since she got her Open University honours degree came through. The courts have agreed to review the decision that life should mean life in her case. The Independent Television News sent a team round to our flat at Chesil Court in Chelsea and interviewed me at 9.30. I figured on *News at Ten*, which was good going on their part.

I was sorry that my new Catholic friend, Ann Widdecombe, appeared on the wrong side of the argument, though I am of course aware that she has always been in favour of capital punishment. For the last week or so the press has been full of her assault on her old chief Michael Howard whom she has accused of misleading the Commons. From the gallery, I heard her speak for forty minutes in the House.

Seeing her there standing amidst her frigid colleagues and cheered by the Labour benches, it was impossible not to regard her as a woman of conscience. But one feels differently about someone's conscience according to whether one agrees with the outcome.

Wednesday May 21, 1997

Four radio programmes before setting off to visit Maria Pearson again at Holloway. I thought that I was bringing her the good news that her appeal had received priority, but she knew it already and being Maria insisted that it was the result of her repeated telephone calls to the commission which now deals with such matters. She gave me credit for making one such call myself.

A rather ludicrous altercation before the interview. I had brought a copy of the House of Lords' *Hansard* for Monday to show her my penal speech. I was forbidden to take it in by various officials. I was aware that I would have to send it to her in any case, but I had never before been refused permission to show a prisoner that document.

The duty governor, a good-looking young lady, new to the job, upheld the ban but she was persuaded by an older male member of the staff to give way, which enabled Maria to read the article. I had quoted the words of Christ that I have quoted so often, 'I was in prison and you came to me.' They appeared to make a deep impression on her.

Thursday May 22, 1997

Delivered an address at the annual meeting of the New Bridge which was celebrating its fortieth anniversary. I was lauded to the skies as the founder to the point where I had to recite the story of the French writer, François Mauriac. He delivered a brilliantly successful defence of Christianity but, as he left the hall, overheard one of the audience saying to another: there goes the imposter.

I told the audience I imagined myself appearing shortly before St Peter. I assumed that I would be hurried along in a queue. I then thought that, like in prison, there would be a glass wall between me and St Peter and we would be shouting at each other.

St Peter: 'Did you do anything useful down there?'

Myself: 'I was a member of the Labour Cabinet.'

St Peter: 'Oh! for God's sake cut out that crap. I asked you, did you do anything useful?'

Myself (more timidly): 'I founded the New Bridge.'

St Peter to an orderly: 'Take this fellow to purgatory and put on his card, "Claims to have founded the New Bridge. Please investigate."'

I told Elizabeth afterwards that it was the most successful speech of my life. She is not likely to check the statement, but I had everything going for me.

Friday May 23, 1997

Visited two prisoners whom I admire and count among my friends, Uday Narayan and Brian Vale. Nobody seems ready to take up Uday's case, and yet among the many prisoners I visit he is one of the few whom I regard as totally innocent of the crime for which he was convicted, namely the murder of his daughter-in-law. What I can't discover, however, is precisely why he was left to defend himself without legal assistance at his trial.

He told me on Friday that he had not dared to cross-examine the main prosecution witness because of threats to his grandson. But I must redouble my efforts in the summer as to how he found himself without legal help.

Monday May 26, 1997

Bank holiday. An expensive visit to Maidstone Prison. On Sundays and bank holidays they have stopped the buses from Maidstone to Hastings, so I went by taxi as I simply had to get there. It was quite an interesting visit.

The prisoner, Colin Davis, was an obviously intelligent man. I have no idea whether he had been a success or failure in life. He sent me the largest collection of material that any prisoner has ever sent me, short of writing a book. He is passionately convinced that the new timetable introduced by the governor at Maidstone is altogether lamentable. The elimination of the half-hour's exercise is only one illustration.

I have since written to the governor telling him that I have received this detailed criticism. I have asked him whether he would like me to send him the material in question, or to take up the matter with the Prison Service headquarters to whom Colin Davis has already complained. I tried to suggest to him tactfully that under the regrettable regime of Howardism he might have introduced a programme which he himself would not welcome.

I am not sure how he will receive my letter. But the issue will not run away when government policy seems as retrograde to prison governors as of course it does to myself.

Wednesday May 28, 1997

Another visit to my friend Father Fred at Wandsworth. He is always in sparkling form when I call, though I fear that he may be more depressed at other times. Andrew McCooey, out of the goodness of his heart, is taking his case against the *News of the World* to the Press Complaints Commission. I would feel that they were bound to come out eventually with a severe criticism of the *News of the World*. But, in my own mind, I do not rule out the possibility of legal action thereafter if the case becomes cut and dried.

Wednesday June 4, 1997

Another visit to Maria Pearson at Holloway. She usually has a fairly well-justified complaint. This time she described her distress at the way in which much of her property had been removed from her cell, as previously indicated, under the new policy of volumetric control.

One rather ludicrous incident I cannot help recalling. I was leaving my coat and bag behind on going into the prison. There was an open cubby hole, and as the prison officer was holding the coat and bag I asked him whether he would mind putting my property into it. He told me that it would be contrary to the rules. On the way out, however, he was kind enough to extract the said property from the cubby hole, so perhaps he thought better of it.

Friday June 6, 1997

Visited Billy Crittenden at Littlehey Prison. Last time I was kept waiting fifty-five minutes, so the visit was ruined. My taxi from Huntingdon (£20 return) was waiting over an hour.

This time I arranged to be picked up an hour and a quarter after the starting point. Billy arrived about twenty minutes after I did. I still can't quite understand why he is considered such a troublesome prisoner that he has to be moved round from prison to prison. I had supposed that it was because he was a first-class boxer and retaliated violently when he was attacked because of his conviction for rape. He insists that this is not the reason. It is because he will never confess that he was guilty and will not therefore attend sex-education classes in prison.

Monday June 9, 1997

An important evening for me in the Lords. I asked the government whether they were ready to reconsider the proposed cuts in the Prison and Probation Services. I was, in effect, asking them to begin to tell us whether they were going to continue with Howardism or return to better ways.

The minister, Lord (Gareth) Williams of Mostyn, the new under-secretary for Home Affairs, a former chairman of the Bar Council, handled the matter discreetly, but gave nothing away. He did indicate, however, that there would be no additional money available in the immediate future, which is bad news in view of the remorseless increase in the number of prisoners. We shall be coming back to these matters again. In the immediate future I intend to concentrate on the proposed twenty-five per cent cut in the Probation Service. Incredible. But the actual prospect at the moment.

Wednesday June 11, 1997

Another visit to Maria Pearson at Holloway. This time she insisted that she has been confined to her cell for twenty-four hours a day for the last two days.

I took up the matter with the governor's excellent secretary, who strongly denied it. I have, therefore, written to the governor and am awaiting a reply.

For the third time my wrist was stamped on the way in, though very half-heartedly. This time I was told, at a slightly higher level, that it was being done because feminists had protested that women were being stamped and not men. There is a tacit agreement that it is a lot of nonsense. I was favourably impressed by the young bustling woman governor who came in at the request of Maria to pursue yet again the removal of some of her property. She did not sit down in the cell till Maria gestured her to a chair.

Sunday June 22, 1997

My week has been made interesting by taking Margaret Thatcher in to lunch at Windsor Castle on Garter Day, and by giving Ann Widdecombe lunch, along with her spiritual advisor (Father) Michael Seed and my daughter Antonia, at the House of Lords.

Wednesday June 25, 1997

Visited my friend Father Fred again. I had heard that the Press Complaints Commission was not ready to accept the complaint about the *News of the World* libel because it was not submitted within a month. They are ready, however, to hear further argument.

Father Fred is still much concerned about the harassment of young Karl Quincey by a gang of half-a-dozen prisoners with a named leader. At his suggestion I saw the governor of the vulnerable wing, who Father Fred told me was a good Christian and a very nice man.

I had a most interesting, if rather depressing, talk with him. He has 280 prisoners on his wing, the vast majority of them sexual offenders. For the first time I realised that sex offenders do not lose their sexual urges when they come to prison and can become a great nuisance to their weaker brethren.

The governor told me that when they have association, there are 240 prisoners in a large room with ten officers supervising. It is impossible to prevent sexual manifestations of some kind, although they are obviously limited. He agreed that the 'leader of the gang' represented the real problem. The governor himself would never interview this man without an officer present, but there is no reason to suppose that any other prison would accept him on a transfer. He promised instead to go on thinking about a transfer for young Quincey. He is not the first governor to whom I have said, 'I am glad that it is you and not I who have to handle these problems.'

Thursday June 26, 1997

Visited Eddie Richardson and Des Nilsen at Whitemoor. Sean Armstrong whom I had met in Wakefield, and is convicted of killing a small girl, had written to me asking me to visit him. The previous day I had confirmed that all three were ready to see me, but when it came to the point, Armstrong sent word that he did not wish for a visit. I must discover why.

Eddie hopes to move very soon to Long Lartin. He had obtained what amounts to apologies from the governor of Whitemoor, though the word 'apology' does not seem to exist in Prison Service vocabulary. He was sent away three times for a month for no genuine reason whatever. He is looking forward to much better prospects at Long Lartin. Seeing him there, I shall be given a good excuse for visiting my sister Mary, who lives nearby.

Des was full of life and his own form of fun. I don't know whether he is worried or not, but a condom which he has possessed for four years in contravention of prison rules has been discovered in his property. I am not quite clear whether he is being charged under prison rules or prosecuted under the criminal law or both. Whichever it is, he is arguing that what he was doing was legal and permissible.

Wednesday July 2, 1997

Visited Maria Pearson once more at Holloway. I am now forced to the conclusion that I can't believe what she tells me, but also that she is so mentally disturbed that she ought to be receiving medical attention. According to her she is now in the punishment block without paper to write on or books.

According to her, she was attacked and punched by one or two prison officers who invaded her cell. As a result she was charged and punished for striking a prison officer. So, I am afraid, it goes on.

I rang the duty officer on Wednesday, and another duty officer on Friday, to record my emphatic opinion that if she can't be transferred to a mental hospital, she ought, at least, to be in the prison hospital. I told them that if a tragedy occurred I would tell a court that I had given the prison fair warning. I have written to the governor this morning to that effect.

Thursday July 3, 1997

Tony Wolf I have mentioned more than once. He is a strange young man aged about twenty-eight, who has been stealing all his life, but he is regarded in prison as a nonce.

I was with him when the news came through that he was being transferred to a prison in Suffolk. He was overjoyed though a little anxious because he will be on 'normal location', that is, not treated as a vulnerable prisoner.

He will be out of prison by September. In some ways he is so intelligent that I wish that I could help him in what must be a very uncertain future.

Tuesday July 8, 1997

Visited, once again, my friend Father Fred. The taxi driver lost his way and I was not as comfortable as I should have been. The visit, therefore, was somewhat abbreviated, but it ended with my promising to write to the chief medical officer about the protection of young Quincey.

It seems to boil down to the need for one or more prison

officers to keep the shower under close observation. As reported earlier, I have already spoken to the wing governor, but Father Fred seems to think that a letter to the chief medical officer might do the trick.

Friday July 11, 1997

Visited Ray Masterman at Brixton. He is a man of many talents, unsuspected by me. For many years he was an inventor, before becoming a fireman and paramedic, and, incidentally, winning high praise for an heroic rescue. He was delighted with the letter I had written to the Home Secretary supporting the legal case against his extradition.

We spent a good deal of time on the dangerous life of vulnerable patients in Brixton. I gather there are about eight including Ray. None of them dares make use of the hour's exercise offered for fear of being attacked.

There would usually be about 200 men on exercise with only three prison officers on duty. Reinforcements would arrive quickly in the event of an attack, but not quickly enough to prevent a prisoner being seriously hurt. I compared the situation in my mind with the vulnerable wing at Wandsworth where ten prison officers have to cope with 240 prisoners on exercise, mostly sex offenders.

In Brixton the attacks would be launched on sexual offenders by other prisoners. In Wandsworth it would be the sexual offenders themselves whose sexual appetite would cause the trouble. I have written to the governor of Brixton begging for safe opportunities for exercise to be provided for the vulnerable prisoners.

Received a poignant letter from Tony Wolf in Belmarsh. He says that on his transfer to an open prison in Suffolk he is to be accompanied by four other prisoners who would know that he is regarded as an informer. He has therefore declined to go and is inevitably in trouble. I have since spoken to a very kindly governor in Belmarsh who says that Tony is his own worst enemy, but he will be treated with proper consideration. I have written to Tony accordingly.

Wednesday July 16, 1997

Since the fall of the Attlee government in 1951 I have opened a good many debates in the House of Lords of one sort or another. In recent years, with a great increase in numbers, they have tended to be unstarred questions at the end of business.

The 'first-time-evers' include the universities, the youth service, equality, prisons, the polytechnics and hospices for the dying. The effect in the long run of such initiatives can never be judged.

In the short run, however, I can fairly describe today's effort as the most successful to date. My motion was to call attention to the cuts in the Probation Service.

Winding up the debate, Lord Gareth Williams reminded us that the Labour government had promised not to increase expenditure for the next two years. But within the total figure there was, of course, room for adjustment. The very effective speeches that followed mine brought out again and again the point that probation is far cheaper than imprisonment, so that from that point of view alone the case for expanding it and reducing the prison population was overwhelming.

I concluded by quoting a weighty speech just delivered by the Lord Chief Justice in favour of alternatives to prison, and a leading article in *The Sun* entitled 'Lock 'Em Up'. I also noted with relief a leading article in the *Daily Mail* entitled 'Jack Straw's U-Turn'. The paper of course denounced it, but I hailed it as a gleam of hope.

The Probation Service is not well organised for fighting

its political battles. I am planning to give evidence to a government committee, just announced, which is to investigate the relationship between the prisons and the Probation Service. David Evans, General Secretary of the Prison Officers' Association, told me off the cuff that he would welcome a fusion between the two services. Harry Fletcher of the National Association of Probation Officers, also off the cuff, was – as I would expect – totally opposed. After all, the Probation Service is a professionally qualified body and the prison officers join their service after a very short period of training.

Nor, I imagine, would those put on probation who had never been in prison be happy with the prison association. But I recall that when I opened the first debate on prisons in 1955 I finished with a plea that prison officers should become social workers.

Wednesday July 30, 1997

Once more visited Uday Narayan and Brian Vale at the Scrubs. I was, I suppose, slightly relieved to find that Uday now intends to spend the next three months working out his case for the European Court and any other relevant authority. He does not expect any action from me until I hear from him again. Indeed, he does not wish to see me again until then, although he assures me, and I believe him, that he greatly enjoys my visits. I still cannot understand how he ever got convicted of murder in the first place.

Friday August 1, 1997

A very instructive morning. I intend concentrating in the immediate future on a study of the Probation Service with a view to giving evidence to the government inquiry into its future. Today I visited the probation office close to Aldgate East tube station in east London, which is in charge of community service orders over a wide area.

The probation officer in charge was highly intelligent and most helpful. He explained that they have 700 men and women on their books, some of them doing as many as 240 hours' community service. Generally speaking, however, the men and women in question do no more than seven hours per week. He reckons that they could do more if more superintending staff could be provided. It strikes me, however, that if most of them are fully employed it might be difficult in any case to fit in more than seven hours.

What I had not realised about community service orders is that the supervisors are not members of the Probation Service, but employed by them as professional instructors.

I have still to work out the actual arrangements made for the 700. I was taken to a workshop where there were no more than a dozen men working. On the face of it that would mean no more than a hundred could be employed during the week. In fact, however, I gathered that there would be many more on Saturdays and possibly Sundays. Also some work would be done in the evening. I'm sure that it all adds up to 700, if one counts in those who work outside without supervision. But, as I say, I can't do the sum at the moment.

I asked how far rehabilitation of the convicted persons was explicitly aimed at, as it is in the case of those based on probation. I was told that in some cases there was a combined order from the court for probation and community service. Otherwise it is hoped and believed that a good measure of rehabilitation is effected by working under discipline.

I asked the young men the rather unfair question whether they were less likely to commit crime in the future as a result of this experience. Not surprisingly, perhaps, they felt sure they would. The probation officer and chief superintendent concurred. I asked him whether his friends were inclined to suppose that community service was a soft option. He said that that was indeed so, but he had no doubt himself that the answer was negative.

Monday August 4, 1997

Half-hour interview on Radio 5. Not more than half of it devoted to penal matters. First question dealt with my general attitude to New Labour. Of course there is a kind of connection between the question I raised in the Lords – whether the party still stands for the redistribution of wealth – and the demand that they should repudiate Howardism. In each case the call is for the party to be loyal to its own traditions.

In this interview I was inevitably questioned about Myra, this time in friendly fashion. I cannot remember saying anything that I had not said often before. Elizabeth and Elizabeth Maxwell both thought my ending particularly good. I was asked how I would like to be remembered. I replied, 'As a loving father, grandfather and great-grandfather, but above all a loving husband.'

The interviewer persisted. 'What about your public life?'

I replied, 'It was said of President Wilson, author of the *League of Nations*, though repudiated at the time by the United States, that Wilson stood weakly for human decency.' That gave Elizabeth a lot of pleasure.

Tuesday August 5, 1997

A valuable visit to Sherborne House, Bermondsey, south London. About thirty adolescent boys aged sixteen to twenty spend ten weeks there at a time. They would otherwise be sent to prison for burglary or robbery.

I was much impressed with the idealism and efficiency of the ladies running the place. I spent an hour or so talking to the inmates, who usually spend four and a half days a week (non-residential) in a kind of group therapy, though it is not officially called therapy. In fact groups of ten or at the most sixteen are assisted by a probation officer to recognise the error of their ways. When they finish the course they remain on probation.

I am entirely favourable to what is being attempted, but I am bound to notice that the numbers involved are very small. I questioned also whether ten weeks was sufficient. I was told by the staff that they thought that it was about the right amount, but I could not help wondering whether if more staff had been available a longer period would have been provided.

Thursday August 7, 1997

Sheila Child, my close friend from our work for the New Bridge, took me to lunch with the former Tory MP Neil Hamilton and his wife Christine. She had, once before, brought me together with them.

I was impressed by two things above all. One, the perfect harmony between the Hamiltons, not so common in the case of those who are in the public doghouse. Two, the positive enthusiasm with which he is looking forward to meeting the Commons' Privileges Committee, hopefully in a televised confrontation. He feels that, for the first time, the public will have a fair chance of judging him.

It is not for me to say whether he is in fact innocent. But I am sure that, by now, he believes totally in his own innocence.

They are an immensely attractive couple. There is nothing I can do to help, but I am happy to think that my moral support has been a real encouragement. I have said that I will try to attend part, at any rate, of the hearing before the committee.

Thursday August 21, 1997

I made my way once more to Wandsworth. There was good news from Father Fred. He has been made chief inspector of work in his part of the prison which, in all the circumstances, is a remarkable tribute to his character and the esteem which he has won by his helpfulness and mental gifts.

Yet he still has plenty of trouble with the occasional prison officer. One of them called him a degenerate the other day. Father Fred reported him and obtained an apology. Quite something and not common in my experience.

I also saw Quincey, that strange young prisoner in whom Father Fred takes what I accept as a fatherly interest. That does not prevent the nasty-minded from calling Quincey, 'Father Fred's Rent Boy'. Nevertheless Quincey seems a lot better in health, although I still think that he should be in a mental hospital rather than prison.

Sunday August 31, 1997

Shattering news arrived early. Not strictly penal, but impossible to ignore in a week just passed. At ten to nine, I was rung up by *The Express* and asked whether Elizabeth, as a royal biographer, would write an article. I asked, 'What about?' The lady at the other end replied, 'Princess Diana, of course.'

Not knowing the awful news, but well aware of the endless gossip about her and Dodi, I replied, 'Diana, isn't that old hat?' Few questions could have been more inappropriate in the circumstances.

But Elizabeth did not feel like writing the kind of thing they wanted. The *Daily Mail* tried later, and when she refused suggested brightly, 'Would you like a ghosted article?' I was frankly shocked at the suggestion. No one I have told this to believes me.

Friday September 5, 1997

Visited Hubert Carnegie in Belmarsh. A slightly mysterious, but charming West Indian. He was convicted of raping a prostitute, which sounds surprising, and of course I only know his own story. Apparently he admits having sex with her, but later hesitated to pay her increased demands and duly found himself convicted of rape. I doubt if there is much that I can do to help him, but of course, as always, I'll do my best when I hear more from him.

Friday October 3, 1997

Denzil Walker at Whitemoor provided even more surprises than the average prisoner. He had written to me to ask my advice about how to proceed against the Home Office over a claim he had against a newsagent near Long Lartin Prison. It turns out that, even on his own account, the newsagent only owed him about £4.

However, he had a further claim against the Home Office over the loss of his property. He has already told me he has won six cases of this character against the Home Office, always representing himself, but this time the case would be heard in some place inaccessible to him.

I promised to take up the matter with the Home Office when I had further details from him. Incidentally he was convicted of murdering a 29-year-old lady, not it seems his girlfriend, by inflicting on her an overdose. Unusually, for someone in his situation, he can provide no reason at all why he did it.

Friday October 17, 1997

I visited Eddie Richardson in Long Lartin. The prison is several miles from Evesham, in Worcestershire, a taxi ride costing £10 each way.

As a prison visitor I encountered some of the same difficulties as at Whitemoor. I am not complaining in either case about being forced to take off my shoes. At Long Lartin they pride themselves on carrying out this little search in a private room. At Whitemoor I have suggested that if they really meant business they would ask me to take off my socks, within which any drug, for instance, could be concealed.

At Long Lartin they did not ask me to remove my socks, but they did feel them, so they had the same thought as I had.

Both at Whitemoor, where I had made a complaint, and at Long Lartin, much time is wasted by their practice of not sending for the prisoner until the visitor enters the waiting room. I suggested at Long Lartin, and the same would apply at Whitemoor, that they would know to bring the prisoner when a visitor had arrived at the visiting centre, which is a good deal earlier. This would mean the Long Lartin objection that visitors often book visits and fail to turn up is irrelevant. At Whitemoor they had another reason for introducing this practice – namely that prisoners could cause trouble if they were assembled waiting for visitors.

Eddie is much happier at Long Lartin than he was at Whitemoor. It seems to be partly a question of personalities. He is naturally keen to come off category A as soon as possible in order to be considered for parole. He obviously thinks that this is much more likely at Long Lartin.

I was very sorry to hear, however, that he is still not

allowed any painting materials in his room and, as there are no art classes, he is therefore not able to paint at all. I am baffled by this restriction at Long Lartin because he was allowed to paint in his room at other high-security prisons such as Parkhurst, Full Sutton near York and Whitemoor. I am writing to the governor.

Monday October 27, 1997

In my unstarred question in the House of Lords, I posed the straightforward dilemma, 'Is the penal policy of the present government going to differ in any respect from that of Michael Howard?' I specifically distinguished the Howardite policies of the last four Conservative years from those of the earlier fourteen.

I began by describing myself as almost obsequiously loyal to the present government. I went on to say that they had been in office for six months. I had visited prisons twice a week during that time and the question mentioned above was pressed on me with increasing urgency and scepticism. As I expected, the answer from the minister was an Irish phrase I have applied to him before: 'Mind you, I said nothing.'

Wednesday October 29, 1997

An hour's debate on Channel 4 on Myra Hindley whose case comes before the Court of Appeal in December. Edward Fitzgerald, her barrister, David Astor, Peter Timms and the former governor of Cookham Wood spoke up very well for Myra, and of course I was quoted doing my bit.

On the other side poor Mrs West (mother of one of the victims, Lesley Ann Downey) was dragged out again. We were told that she was suffering from cancer and no one could fail to be profoundly sorry for her. Right up to the end I was not sure whether the programme had been fair to Myra. But when David Astor was given an effective last word, I felt they had been.

Thursday October 30, 1997

At last *The Sun* published my article in favour of Myra. They had taken a good deal of trouble to make my contribution into an effective piece of journalism. I give them credit for that and for publishing a good up-to-date photograph of Myra.

But the heading at the top of the page speaks for itself: 'The *Sun* Special on the Most Evil Woman of All Time'. 'Whosoever sups with the devil must use a long spoon' springs to mind, but this is an occasion when the supping seems to me to have been worthwhile.

Wednesday November 5, 1997

Visited Father Fred at Wandsworth, a fortnightly pleasure. This time the pleasure was somewhat diluted. When I arrived, the officer at the window told me bluntly that he had nothing booked for me. I had, in fact, booked visits to Karl Quincey and Father Fred the day before.

The officer telephoned the office dealing with legal visits, which also insisted that nothing had been booked. This was the first time in all these years there seemed a real danger that I would be refused entry. However, I am too old to be shaken off quite so easily. Eventually the visits governor (a new appointment) arrived on the scene and arranged for me to see Father Fred. There was only time left, after a lot of argument, for the one visit.

Father Fred was pleased to tell me that, partly because of my intervention, Quincey was receiving more medical attention. At my request Governor Davis had seen both him and Father Fred, but, in the latter case, had not been effective so far. Father Fred had been reduced to a basic status which meant that he spent almost the whole day in his cell.

His alleged offence appears to be some active insubordination. According to him, the prison officer in question has developed a grudge against him. I am trying to reach Governor Davis to return to the matter. So far I have been unlucky.

Father Fred is now able to say his own Mass, well attended, I gather, in particular by Filipinos.

Thursday November 6, 1997

Visited a protégé of my good friend Ben Farrer at Littlehey Prison. Ben is, to say the least, an unusual man and lived up to his reputation on this occasion.

He had begged me to visit a prisoner he called Daniel Brown, though when I asked him how to address him he said, 'Call me Stanley.' Daniel Stanley had been Ben's lodger, and was in Ben's eyes his adopted son. I had agreed to meet Ben at The Wheatsheaf and walk over to the prison nearby together. With some trouble I obtained a visiting order for Ben, though as a member of a House of Parliament I do not require one.

No sign of Ben at The Wheatsheaf, no sign of Ben at the prison.

Daniel Stanley is aged twenty-three, a pleasant young man who had not been in trouble before and expects to be all right when he comes out. His offence was arson, the sentence four years reduced to two. He told me that he was drunk at the time.

I invited him and his girlfriend, if he has one at the time, to come to tea at the House of Lords when he emerges next June.

Next morning I rang Ben, who was full of gratitude for the visit. He seemed to think, however, that his absence was easily explained. He was sitting on a wonderful mahogany seat in the lavatory of his house in Cambridge when the taxi arrived. He was slow to finish the operation. By the time he went to the door the taxi had gone. Considering the taxi was losing a twenty-mile-each-way job it is all rather mysterious. But so are many things connected with Ben.

A footnote to the visit. Enjoying a sandwich and a drink in The Wheatsheaf, I had an interesting conversation with a lady doing educational work in the prison. She expects to lose her job in April because of the savage cuts in prison education. I made a firm resolution to pursue this issue in any way open to me. But what was significant was that her son, aged twenty-five, a teacher in a school of some kind, was unsympathetic to prisoners and thought that they had too good a time.

So there you have encapsulated the far-reaching problem of cuts confronting Jack Straw: on the one hand a policy condemned by anyone with serious knowledge of prisons; on the other hand an intelligent member of the public, probably agreeing with that policy, even though he damaged his mother.

Wednesday November 12, 1997

Set out to visit Brian Vale and Billy Crittenden at the Scrubs. Proceedings far from smooth. When I arrived an officer told me, deadpan, 'I have bad news I am afraid. Your visit has been refused by Vale.'

On further enquiry I discovered that he had to begin a new education course and would like to see me on another occasion. I am afraid that the way the news was broken to me is somewhat typical of prison language. I then said, 'What about Crittenden?' They said, 'We haven't got any visit booked for Crittenden.' Next time I must keep the telephone message in which I am informed that certain visits have been confirmed.

However, Billy was produced in due course and we had, as always, a pleasant talk. He seems to have discarded the idea that the uncle of the young woman who got him convicted of rape should interrogate her with the help of a concealed tape recorder. He still believes, however, that the uncle could give valuable evidence on his behalf, because he would be able to tell a court how certain information came to him from the girl's mother.

It was, apparently, the girl's mother who told the girl that Billy was already married, hence her cry of rape. But it seems that she had this information available the last time they had sex together. What follows is obscure, but after talking to Billy for some time she rushed out and made the accusation. My own surmise is that something infuriated her in the conversation following the sex act, hence she became at once the woman scorned.

Friday November 14, 1997

Scrubs again. Brian Vale was his usual ebullient self. He apologised for not being available on Wednesday, explaining that he was only told that I was coming that morning. I am afraid that this happens all too often. I always ask to be assured that the prisoner is ready and willing to see me. Sometimes the staff seem to give the assurance without verification.

I was glad to meet Uday Narayan again. I sometimes wonder whether he fails to make himself understood. When I last saw him, he told me that he did not wish to see me for three months because he was too busy with his case. I am still not sure whether he really meant it. At any rate we are back as friends though it does not seem that I can assist his appeal to Europe. For one reason or another he never seems able to obtain sufficient legal advice. I remain convinced of his innocence.

My third prisoner was Curtis Howard, a six-foot-tall black American. Again, I doubt if I can be of any use to him, but he seemed to appreciate the visit. He pleaded guilty some time ago to the manslaughter of a white girlfriend in England, and then departed quickly to America.

He was eventually extradited back and his plea of manslaughter was accepted. He received a life sentence. It was quite a light tariff, six years, but he insists that the two years he spent on remand in America should be deducted.

So far, however, only one has been deducted, on the grounds that he delayed extradition unnecessarily. I am, of course, sympathetic but open-minded on the issue.

Tuesday December 18, 1997

A rather hectic day. At 9.45 a.m. I reported to the Law Courts where the Lord Chief Justice and his two colleagues were about to deliver judgment on Myra's appeal against 'life meaning life'. The Lord Chief Justice was not, of course, asked to say whether Jack Straw's confirmation of that sentence was just or unjust, but only whether it was lawful. In the event he announced that it was lawful, but only because the possibility was left open for an appeal if she could prove exceptional progress. Michael Howard had not left such a loophole and had, therefore, been acting illegally.

All that makes pretty good nonsense in the case of Myra, who has already been recommended by the Parole Board for an open prison. But it is good news all the same. That apart, leave to appeal was granted. The case will now, apparently, go to the Appeal Court and, if necessary, to the House of Lords, and again, if necessary, to Europe.

There was a rumour that the Lord Chief Justice and his colleagues recognised the justice of the appeal, but did not want a real showdown with the government. Be that as it may, he expressed disquiet about the present situation and felt that there should be further investigation of whether these decisions should be taken by the Home Secretary or the judiciary. So, on balance, it was a plus morning.

On leaving the court I was besieged by journalists and television representatives. I talked and talked, then and later. I am glad that *The Guardian* reported me saying, 'this takes us halfway to capital punishment'. I am glad too that the *Evening Standard* quoted my quotation from Pastor Bonhoeffer: 'This is not the end but the beginning.'

3.15 p.m. Visited Curtis Howard at Wormwood Scrubs again. I am entirely sympathetic to him as an attractive intellectual man, but I am at least as interested as him in the question as to whether he can get his tariff reduced. He tells me that five prisoners serving life in the Scrubs have had reductions in their tariffs. I should add that I have taken up Curtis Howard's claim with the Home Secretary.

Sunday December 28, 1997

It is just worth reporting, perhaps, my exchanges with the editor of *The Sun*. On Saturday of last week they had a second leading article headed 'Wrongford'. They said that I had been talking rot about Myra for twenty years and advised me to consult with the parents of the country.

Last Tuesday I called the editor. He seemed to be in an advanced state of excitement. 'I am not going to have you abusing my staff,' he shouted. 'I'll never print another word you write. You're a pompous idiot. OK? OK?'

I said, 'Not OK at all – crap! crap!' I am certainly hoping to get the gist of my letter in response to the leading article published somewhere. Fortunately that afternoon I ran into the former Labour deputy leader, Roy Hattersley, who has recently supported Myra's case on the radio. I handed him my letter. He did not expect to use it in his weekly column in *The Guardian*, but he hoped that it would see the light of day somehow.

Monday December 29, 1997

Made my fortnightly visit to Father Fred. He had sent me a letter which he wanted me to send to the Minister for Prisons, Joyce Quinn, mainly about his maltreatment in the prison by two officers whom he named. I pressed him on the question of whether it would really benefit him or simply arouse their further enmity. He does not wish a transfer to another prison, nor is he asking for them to be transferred. He is convinced, however, that he would be better treated if they are aware that the Minister for Prisons has her eye on them.

I am glad that, in his letter to the minister which I have now forwarded with my support, he mentions the kindness of his wing governor, Mr Davis, who, I am sorry to say, is soon to retire.

Wednesday December 31, 1997

Made a return visit to Long Lartin to see Eddie Richardson. On the last occasion, I left without seeing him because of the obstruction of staff. This time I arranged to come back by a somewhat later train, which was just as well even though my entry went like clockwork. This may have been due to the complaint recorded in my letter to the deputy governor of December 21, to which, incidentally, I have not yet had a reply. The secretary to the governor was also very helpful, suggesting that I should arrive at 1.30 and leave any questionable material (magnifying glass, money over £15, etc.) at the visiting centre.

What was interesting was that three of the procedures insisted on last time were not imposed on this occasion. My shoes were not removed, nor was my belt, and I was not asked to put out my tongue. A difficult question arises – were they wrong last time or this time? They can hardly have been right both times. I am writing to the Director-General of the Prison Service asking for an interview with one of his staff before putting down a further question in the House of Lords.

Friday January 2, 1998

I was due to visit Curtis Howard and Brian Vale at the Scrubs. Transport failure made it impossible. So I took the opportunity of visiting Jasminko Cerkezovic, in Brixton, who has no one to visit him. After six years on a charge of rape which he vigorously denies, he is in great danger of being extradited to France on a charge of attempted murder, which he denies just as vigorously.

He told me that his mother was murdered by the next-door neighbour in Sarajevo. He belonged to a Croatian minority there who, in the event, suffered terrible persecution from the Serb majority.

His solicitor is anxious to find out whether Cerkezovic could offer any suggestions about the identity of those who had attempted the murder. He could only inform me that the man in question was a criminal, and that the attempt might have been made in some criminal connection. He is an attractive man facing a painful future with much courage.

Wednesday January 7, 1998

Visited Des Nilsen again in Whitemoor. In an earlier meeting I once said to him, 'You're a bit arrogant, aren't you Des?' And he replied, 'If you were called a monster and somehow had to survive you might have to seem a bit arrogant.' I'm not sure whether he remembered that conversation, but at one point he said on Wednesday, 'I suppose you think I'm a bit arrogant.' I couldn't deny that the thought had passed through my mind, but I also understood a possible explanation.

He had written me a ten-page letter complaining of his maltreatment in recent times. I told him that I would gladly raise any concrete issue with the governor. After a long discussion he agreed to write a two-page letter for me to support. I am bound to say that as between him and the staff I would not know where to lay the responsibility for difficult relations, but he does genuinely seem to have been treated badly recently.

The better news is his friend Mark has eventually rescued Des's autobiography from the solicitor who had, apparently, to be paid £3,000 to release it. I have promised Des to take up the possibility of publication with my literary agent Mike Shaw.

Des is indeed a strange man, but not by any means devoid of moral sense. He tells me that he would not wish to come out of prison if it offended the relatives of his victims. This is how people sometimes say Myra ought to feel. But no friend of hers would ever tell her that it is her duty. Indeed, when you think of the enormous expense of keeping someone in prison, it is not a rational idea. Nevertheless it does Des credit. I told him that I did not agree with him, but I admired him for this desire to make atonement (my phrase not his).

Friday January 9, 1998

Visited Curtis Howard and Brian Vale once more in the Scrubs. They are both making representations about a reduction in their own tariff, encouraged by the fact that the Home Secretary, Jack Straw, is now allowing representations about exceptional progress.

I promised in each case three things. One, that I would be happy to meet the prisoner's solicitor in the House of Lords whenever he wanted to see me. Two, I would write any letter of support that the solicitor thought would be useful. Three, I would appear in person to give evidence to character or accompany the solicitor to any official concerned with the case. I suggested to Curtis that it would be useful if I could see one of the essays he had written in the course of his studies in the prison. Both of them have done several further education courses.

Tuesday January 13, 1998

Another visit to Father Fred, enjoyable as always. It seems that the letter that I wrote at his request to Joyce Quinn, Minister for Prisons, has borne fruit. There has been a general improvement in his situation. He has been rescued from 'basics', a kind of punishment which restricted his life quite seriously. He is still waiting for an operation and is writing a letter to me to be forwarded with support to the medical authorities.

Friday January 16, 1998

I had hoped to go to the trial of Jasminko Cerkezovic, but my sister Pansy arrived from Rome – ninety-three years old, but a year or two older than myself. Andrew McCooey told me later that Cerkezovic will now face extradition to France on a charge of attempted murder.

I hope to visit him before he leaves England. Andrew says he has been encouraged by my visits. Except for Andrew, he seems to have no one in the world to back him up. It is difficult to believe that he could really be guilty of shooting someone two or three times in the head.

Thursday January 22, 1998

Visited Cerkezovic at Brixton. What a life he has led. Five years in the French Foreign Legion, including action in various parts of the world, and somewhere along the line acquiring a knowledge of several languages including Russian.

We have become close. He asked me if there was any chance of my coming to speak for him at his trial in France. I had to decline; my knowledge of French would not make me effective in a French court. I promised, however, that I would write a strong letter of support saying that I had come to know him well and was convinced that he was a thoroughly honest man. Once again I admire his fortitude, which I would certainly not have equalled in his case.

Friday January 23, 1998

Another visit to Curtis Howard and Brian Vale in the Scrubs. Both are serving discretionary life sentences for manslaughter. I am opening a debate on February 18 on the need to put mandatory life prisoners on the same footing as discretionary ones. I told them both, therefore, that I had my own selfish reasons for wanting to interrogate them.

These two very intelligent discretionary life prisoners brought home to me the fact that their situation raises problems of its own. They had their tariffs fixed by the courts. Although, as the Lord Chief Justice said, the time they spend in prison is determined by the judiciary, not the executive, they are not able to approach their quasi-judicial panel until their tariff has expired. If they wish to get their tariff reduced, they have to go to the Home Office, that is, the executive. I leave the complications there for the moment.

Time is always too short to pursue all the points that Brian Vale and I could debate. I told him about my recent attendance at the memorial service for Isaiah Berlin. No one of my generation was more popular. The synagogue was packed with Jews and non-Jews. Isaiah himself was described as a secular Jew by the Chief Rabbi, which presumably meant that he did not accept the Jewish religion. But nothing could have been more Jewish than the arrangements. The women were severely separated from the men. We were told that Isaiah wanted the service to be there because, when his parents arrived in England with him as a small boy from Riga, that is where they worshipped.

Brian Vale is passionately Jewish, but also Marxist. He said that he fully understood why Isaiah wanted to be commemorated there. I was left uncertain whether he would make the same choice when his time came.

Wednesday January 28, 1998

Another entertaining visit to Father Fred. I told him that if only he would rejoin the official Catholic Church I would like to go to him for confession. I have longer talks about religion with him than with anyone else at the moment and always I benefit, although, of course, he is intensely traditional and opposed, for example, to women priests.

Incidentally, Father Fred is happy to tell me that two of the prison officers who were hostile to him have been moved out of the prison and the other two are giving him no trouble. He persuades me that my letter to Joyce Quinn, Minister for Prisons, has borne fruit.

Thursday January 29, 1998

Visited, at his request, a prisoner in Kingston Prison, Portsmouth, new to me – James Berry, aged sixty-seven, grey-haired, rather handsome, slightly overweight. He could be mistaken, dressed otherwise, for an hereditary peer. When not in prison, he has been a landscape gardener, quite successful I think. He composes music and plays the organ in the chapel.

All that sounds most respectable. But his record is, to say the least, colourful. Forty-two years ago he divorced his wife, who retained custody of their baby. When the child was twenty-one months old, my new friend was so unhappy about its condition that he gassed the child to death and attempted to do likewise to himself. He survived and was convicted of murder. This was 1955, so he was sentenced to death by hanging with a recommendation for mercy.

He was liberated after nine years and married again, having two children. Unfortunately he was convicted of offences against adolescent boys and went to prison for quite a long time. This second wife divorced him, but they remain on good terms and the children visit him.

Liberated again he married a much younger woman of South American stock. He found her impossible and divorced her, after having two more children by her. She acquired a boyfriend and, after a while, she took him to court for seeing their two children more often than was permitted.

He has now been five years in prison without, of course, any trial. So there it is. Three marriages. One dead child. Four living ones. Three incarcerations, with a life sentence still hanging over him, whose conditions he failed to comply with when he last emerged from prison.

He did admit to one big nervous breakdown on the way and maybe has had more than one. I found him most agreeable and told him that I knew another prisoner (David Rundle) who puts up with the same kind of maltreatment through the machinery of recall.

I have made unsuccessful efforts to get that improved through legislation. In the event I got on to his solicitor who is going to write a letter to the Minister for Prisons, Joyce Quinn, which I will warmly support. I am bound to say that he described the over-sixties' unit as quite pleasant, but naturally he yearns for freedom – to which, in my opinion, he is now entitled.

Wednesday February 4, 1998

Visited Michael Bettaney at Swaleside Prison, after an interval of I can't think how many years. Michael Bettaney must count as one of the most interesting prisoners I have ever visited.

He was, and is again, a Catholic, but in between became a communist and was convicted as a spy, receiving twenty-three years. After graduating at Oxford he was working for an advanced degree when attracted into MI5 or MI6, I am not quite sure which. He was so disgusted with their undercover methods in Northern Ireland, for example, that he rushed to the other extreme and embraced the communist cause. His career as a spy did not last long because he was exposed to the authorities by a Russian double agent.

Years ago, when I first visited him in prison, he had returned to the church and was thinking of becoming a monk. He discontinued our visits because they attracted undue publicity (Myra has felt the same). He continued to send me Christmas cards and recently invited me to visit him again.

At the worst he hoped to be out of prison by the beginning of 1989. He would have obtained parole long ago, but the security services regard him as public enemy number one because he knows so many of their secrets. However, they can't stop him coming out after he has served fifteen of the twenty-three years.

He was as bright as ever, though looking rather like a man who has survived a long illness. He is very happy in the thought that when he is released his fiancée will be waiting for him. He faces the fact, however, that he will be labelled a traitor for the rest of his life and must go about the world, in my expression, with lowered eyes.

Sunday February 15, 1998

Very little on the penal front this week. Last week I had a fall and damaged my leg, though nothing, I am assured, was broken. I am making steady progress, but paid only one visit, to Father Fred on Friday.

He insists that I am of real service to him in making a fuss on his behalf repeatedly. I am happy to take his word for it. He has been waiting three years for a hernia operation, but he assures me that my representations to the medical authorities seem likely to bear fruit.

His main complaint at the moment is that all outside exercise has apparently been eliminated by the new governor. The reasons are obscure, but he seems anxious to make Wandsworth more of a working prison. When I receive a letter from Father Fred, I shall be writing to the governor. He is a Catholic from Northern Ireland of the old school.

Father Fred gave me a dramatic account of life in the sex offenders' re-education class. Recently he was stretched out on the floor in front of the class while an eighteen-stone prisoner was suspended above him. This was intended to bring home to him the feelings of a victim being threatened with rape. He has a very keen sense of humour which enables him to extract an element of amusement from these painful happenings. His instructor complains that he does not burst into tears like some of the other prisoners as a sign of repentance. He has been assured by his probation officer that he is felt to be making satisfactory progress.

Wednesday February 18, 1998

I visited Roy in the Royal Free Hospital in Hampstead. I had persuaded him and Dr King, his eminent psychiatrist, that he ought to return to hospital for a time at least. Neither was very keen on the idea, but it certainly did no harm.

He had isolated himself in his flat – refusing to see anybody. And yet not long before he came to tea with Lady Brocklebank, a doctor, who had begun to employ him as a chauffeur – the best job I can remember him having. I heard at one moment from a friend of hers that he was very depressed, and soon afterwards I learnt that he had left her service. The circumstances remain mysterious.

I was allowed to give him lunch in the public house near the hospital. He was as depressed as I have ever seen him, mentioning suicide, and refusing to meet other friends. He showed much concern for my earlier accident, but otherwise seemed to take no interest in anything or anybody.

When I left him I rang Dr King and reported on his sad condition. But by now he has been released from hospital where he was a voluntary patient. Dr King told me that there was a terrible shortage of beds. I could only reply that he had chosen an arduous profession and wished him well.

In the evening I opened a debate in the Lords. I called on the government to consider transferring from the Home Secretary to the judiciary the decisions as to the length of time mandatory life prisoners remain in custody. Mandatory life prisoners, at the moment numbering about 3,000, have been convicted of murder. Another 400 to 500 discretionary life prisoners have been convicted of manslaughter or, for example, repeated sexual offences.

In the end ten speakers took part. The official Conservative spokesman and the government minister stood by the present arrangement for mandatory life prisoners. But the other seven speakers supported my proposition, though one of them provoked me into interruption, when he told the House that Myra Hindley would be killed if she were released.

I was lucky to be able to produce some helpful quotations. *The Sun* newspaper called Myra Hindley the most evil woman who had ever lived. A taxi driver told me recently that he had four children and feared for their safety if she came out of prison. I asked him what, if anything, he knew about her. He replied, what he read in *The Sun*.

On the other hand, Peter Timms, former governor of Maidstone Prison, now a Methodist minister, and a series of Catholic priests, have all testified to her good character. A priest who had charge of her for four years in Cookham Wood Prison described her as a caring, sensitive and intelligent person.

She is only one of 3,000 mandatory life prisoners, but she provided a telling example of the dilemma confronting the Home Secretary. Should he do what was right or should he try to satisfy the emotions of the multitude? The opinion has frequently been expressed that no Home Secretary would dare to let her out. It is high time that Home Secretaries were rescued from this dilemma.

I used the additional argument that discretionary life prisoners were allowed to appear before the Parole Board and be represented there. A judge presided over it and the decisions were binding. Mandatory life prisoners depended on correspondence with the Home Office. No meaningful reasons were given when release was refused.

I was very happy with the outcome of the debate.

Wednesday February 25, 1998

Only one prison visit this week. My leg is recovering rather slowly. I expect to make up for it in the coming week.

As usual I have had interesting talks with Curtis Howard and Brian Vale in the Scrubs. Both are highly intellectual, though not professorial like my friend Father Fred. Both are pleased that I mentioned them, though not by name, in the recent speech in the House of Lords.

Sunday March 1, 1998

Attended Mass, as for the last three weeks, in the Village Hall near Bernhurst. Our Catholic church was vandalised and part of it set on fire – accidentally, it was charitably surmised. I am told that it was done by boys, though no one seems to have seen them, let alone caught them. One is left asking oneself what one would do to fifteen-year-olds if they could be arrested and convicted.

The dilemma of whether or not to take them away from home and install them in some kind of institution would present itself. My own solution, which does not seem likely to be adopted, is to set up a number of correctional day schools. If they were local boys that would mean, presumably, going to Hastings with all the transport problems involved.

Wednesday March 4, 1998

Made my way for the first time for a good many years to Ashworth Special Hospital on Merseyside. Ian Brady had asked me to come, and, after repudiating me and calling me (allegedly) a 'Home Office lackey', he could not be denied a visit. Mercifully the hospital sent a charming senior nurse to take me from Liverpool to Ashworth and back.

I had an hour's interview with Ian. He was wearing dark glasses and speaking with a Scottish accent, which I had forgotten, but he was still the same old Ian. He wanted to lecture me, and indeed anyone else prepared to listen, on all that was going wrong at Ashworth. I kept interrupting to discover what he thought I could do to help.

At the end of the interview I asked whether he felt able to thank me for coming. He did not reply. Later, however, he joined me in the nurses' room and became much more friendly. At the end he got up and shook hands and said, 'thanks'. The next day he wrote me a long letter which ended with the words, 'Thank you for the visit.' He is not the first prisoner who has, in my experience, a problem with saying, 'thank you'. I always recall the words of Richard Nixon: 'I've screwed everything up. I've let everyone down, but I am not going to grovel.'

Thursday March 5, 1998

Through the generosity of Antonia's husband, Harold Pinter, my daughter Rachel and I were able to visit Woodhill Prison near Milton Keynes by car. It took us just under an hour after arrival to meet the prisoner we had come to visit. (I filed a complaint accordingly.)

This was my old friend Charlie Bronson, recently described on television as the most dangerous criminal in England. Yet I was told at the prison, as in other prisons, that Charlie is popular and respected. Feared, I suppose one would have to add, in view of his tendency to take governors and others hostage.

He was in excellent form. Rachel, as joint editor of *Inside Time*, a prisoners' paper, was in a good position to ask him to contribute to it. At the moment he is concentrating on cartoons. I am sure that he will send her some.

He is also an entertaining writer, but is involved with a lady in America called Angela who is writing a kind of transatlantic novel with him. My granddaughter Rosie Billington, a literary agent, regards him as a much more entertaining writer than his American partner.

There was only one tense moment. Suddenly he got the idea that one of the guards was standing too close to him and obstructing his vision. A flare-up seemed imminent, but then we all cooled down.

Thursday March 12, 1998

Visited once more my friend Father Fred. I was puzzled, but not seriously upset, by the news on the previous Friday that he had refused to see me. I had booked a visit for three o'clock and arrived at 3.15. But I gather that he and other prisoners were brought over at a quarter to one, and by 3.15 it was concluded that I was not coming.

He had a horrifying tale to tell about a young prisoner, aged twenty-two – a sexual offender, though not, I think, convicted of the most serious crimes. He was going to leave prison in a fortnight's time, but after reading the tabloid press was so terrified of the lynching that he was likely to receive that he hanged himself. Father Fred heard the chair dropping in the neighbouring cell. He was, it seems, maltreated by two of the same officers who had tried to bully Father Fred.

Friday March 13, 1998

Attended a remarkable gathering at Wandsworth. A large crowd of prisoners heard a spellbinding speech by my old friend Bob Tierney, delivered without notes.

It lasted an hour. Bob spoke in what you can only call working-class prison jargon, and got right to the hearts of his audience. He has the double qualification of being an ex-prisoner, and being a remarkable speaker in the old-fashioned open-air style.

One unpleasant question was asked, which drew rather too much applause for my liking: why are sex offenders treated better than we are? (I must find out some time whether the vulnerable-wing prisoners, including Father Fred, were separately seated.) By and large it was a tremendous success. But I was left realising that it is one thing to help prisoners from the outside, another from long experience of the ordeal.

Wednesday March 18, 1998

I had my usual very pleasant visits to Curtis Howard and Brian Vale at the Scrubs. Two very stimulating men.

Curtis Howard is about to be transferred to Portland Prison in the United States so I shall not expect to see him again. He has promised to keep in touch with me by letter. I shall always think of this tall distinguished-looking black man with affection.

Brian was his usual sparkling self. He is a very shrewd judge of politics and, in particular, a discerning critic of the present government from an old-fashioned socialist position. But I shall keep asking him how employment is to be provided under his form of socialism.

Friday March 27, 1998

Visited Father Fred and found him looking quite a lot younger after his long-awaited operation. As usual he had a tale of mixed good treatment and bad. He had been wonderfully well looked after at the hospital, but when he came back to the prison he had to wait eight hours in reception. Two governors had come to apologise. The fact that they were not able to alleviate his plight is some indication of the extraordinary incoherence of arrangements in prison.

I am, at his request, writing to the governor about this, and also in a more careful way about the problem of giving him adequate exercise. I am to thank the governor for making good arrangements for the next two months, but beyond that, who knows?

I asked Father Fred for his views on purgatory. For example, what of the many criminals who die unrepentant? Surely he does not want them to go to hell? Up until now he has preferred in his replies to me to rely on the infinite mercy of God. As I think they say in modern journalism – watch this space.

Monday March 30, 1998

Visited Belmarsh to see Ray Masterman, shortly to be extradited to America where it seems all too likely that he will serve fifteen years for the alleged rape of a girl of eight whom he was attending as a paramedic.

Even by prison-visiting standards, I had a bad time getting in. I was told that the visit began at two. I arrived at 1.50 and saw the prisoner more than three-quarters of an hour later. The details need not detain us. One example is enough. At the first point of call I was registered as a visitor, but not given any badge or sign of acceptance. At the fifth point of call the officer held matters up for a good ten minutes because I had no such badge. He later told me that if I had said at the beginning I was Lord Longford he would have let me in.

When I had finished my visit to the prisoner I asked to see a duty governor to make a complaint. A charming youngish woman arrived and obviously stirred things up.

When I returned to my first point of call the row was going on the telephone between the officer who had not given me the badge and the later officer who had demanded it. I heard, 'Well everyone knows Lord Longford.'

Masterman was, considering everything, quite cheerful. He was very anxious to see someone from the Foreign Office to explain his plan to deal with the threat of anthrax presented by Saddam. I promised to write about it without any expectation of anything happening.

Monday April 6, 1998

Set off to visit my friend Father Fred in Wandsworth, with paedophiles very much on my mind. The word has suddenly become all too popular, or rather unpopular. It is used in all sorts of misleading ways. One extreme are serial child killers. At the other, some like the much-loved Catholic priest who was suspended for a time from his parish for fondling a seventeen-year-old boy twenty-five years earlier.

Matthew Parris has done a useful job in his column in *The Times* in protesting against the lynch-mob hysteria. But much clarification is necessary before any wise measures can be adopted. Just before I set off for Wandsworth the papers were full (and remain full) of a certain Sidney Cooke, a child killer just released from Wandsworth the day before my journey. He had served nine years of a sixteen-year sentence for the manslaughter of a child, but he is a man of seventy with a long string of offences.

I am left with these conclusions. Where a mental factor can be agreed upon by doctors, the offender should go to some kind of mental institution. Otherwise, where the crimes are sufficiently grave, a life sentence should be passed of a discretionary character, leaving it to a judicial panel to decide when the prisoner should be released.

Father Fred was grateful to the governor of Wandsworth for apologising in writing for the way he was kept waiting without medication for eight hours after his operation. But he is still anxious that I should return to the issue of exercise. The temporary permission now seems to have ended.

Tuesday April 7, 1998

Visited Brian Vale in Wormwood Scrubs again. As always we had a stimulating talk about Labour policy, but this time I was more interested in the ways in which he felt that he had benefited from 'treatment' in prison.

He felt that he had been assisted to face up to his own weaknesses, not just the crime, but the weaknesses of character that had made it possible. He is looking forward to going to Grendon Underwood at Aylesbury and to taking part in group therapy.

He admitted, however, that many prisoners found it far more difficult to come clean in this way. This issue is related, obviously, to that of remorse, which is expected of prisoners while not expected of the rest of us.

Friday April 17, 1998

Visited two prisoners new to me. The story of Philip Portington is extraordinary. He paid a holiday visit to Greece with a party of friends. They met another English tourist and later, when they returned to England, heard that he had been murdered with a knife.

Philip Portington went out the following year to the same place without any problem arising, though I learnt later from his solicitor that he went out under an alias. He went out again the following year and was arrested for the murder of the English tourist.

Subsequently he spent twelve years in a Greek jail (his solicitor said that he was tortured, though Philip did not mention it to me). He had been in Wandsworth for a month. He has been given a seventeen-year tariff by the British authorities as a condition of his return to England. But there are many aspects of his case which are most unsatisfactory.

I am convinced of his innocence, if only because no one who has committed a murder in Greece would go back to the same place two years running. I look forward to asking him, 'Why an alias, on the first occasion at least?' when I visit him next.

The other prisoner was Lee McGregor who had written to me asking me to visit him. He was full of charm, aged thirty, with very long curly black hair. He is serving a sentence of eleven years for rape and attempted murder. He pleaded guilty at the trial, but has no idea whether he did or didn't do the things he is accused of. He is a recognised schizophrenic, but told me that he had not been warned that he must not combine the drugs he takes for that with alcohol. On the occasion in question he combined the two (in good measure I expect) and had no idea what he did subsequently.

The young woman whom it seems he raped and tried to murder was someone he met in the street and against whom he could not possibly have had any grudge. He is very likeable and I am much impressed by the fact that he recognises that, when at large, he could be dangerous to society. He would like to be transferred to a mental hospital for a time at least. I promised to take up the matter on his behalf.

Monday April 20, 1998

Made my way to Kent and the Medway Training Centre for twelve- to fourteen-year-olds. I was entertained to lunch by the very impressive director, a young woman who has had a lot of experience in local government secure units. Unfortunately, perhaps, three gentlemen were present from Group 4, the security company to whom the government has contracted out the centre. I did not learn much from them, but they may have slightly inhibited the director.

When in full operation, it is expected that there will be one hundred staff and forty inmates, who will be called trainees. The latter will be persistent offenders, mostly young thieves I fancy, but not authors of serious crimes.

At present one hundred staff are on the payroll and two trainees have arrived. I have a question down for the Lords tomorrow, asking how the cost per trainee at the centre compares with the cost per child or young person in local government secure units. The reason for the question is obvious. But I must try to use the occasion to express dislike of the whole idea of placing these children under the Home Office which means that they will be labelled as criminals for life.

On a lighter note I am very dependent in these latter days on a reasonable dose of alcohol in the middle of the day. To get to the centre I had to travel from Bernhurst to Chatham (two railway changes on the way) and then after lunch to the House of Lords and then back to Sussex, as Elizabeth was not well. At Chatham I asked for sherry at the buffet, but was not surprised to find that they did not stock it. I settled for whisky and ginger ale, and also bought two small bottles of wine. I asked for white, but had to put up with red.

I produced them from my pocket at lunch and offered one to the director in front of her three employers. She naturally could not accept one, so I gratefully drank them both.

Wednesday April 22, 1998

Visited Broadmoor as part of Peter Thompson's entourage. A special lunch was being given for him and others involved with the Matthew Trust of which I have the honour to be president. It was a lovely occasion for all of us, not least because the tributes to Peter were so well justified. The chairman and the chief executive were both attractive women.

Following my tribute to the director of the new Medway Centre I am asking myself whether women are better than men in control of some kinds of social service. I realise that I am thinking primarily of their handling of male patients and offenders. I must ask an experienced woman whether they are equally good in control of women.

I first visited Broadmoor in 1940, and visited Peter in his years there as a prisoner between 1965 and 1969 along with various occasions since. I don't know that I learnt anything new on this occasion, except that there are 1,200 staff to deal with 450 patients and that there are 100 patients whom the chairman and chief executive do not consider need such high security. They are not transferred out because suitable accommodation is not available. Meanwhile there are long waiting lists at the special hospitals.

The obvious answer is to build more medium-security hospitals. But this clearly costs a lot of money, so no solution is likely in the near future.

I was glad to meet a number of patients at the lunch provided for us. One had been at Eton and then in Broadmoor for sixteen years. He was quite sorry to leave. Indeed the same was true of the other patients I spoke to. But I suppose I might be told that the patients in question were selected as management friendly.

When I heard that the average length of stay was eight years I naturally began wondering how fit the average patient was for release after that period. No perfect answer is likely to be available. But I was happy to learn that the chief executive, herself a professional psychiatrist, had considerable experience of dealing with former inmates.

Peter revealed in his speech what I had not clearly known before – that he had tried to avoid leaving Broadmoor. Since then he has not only been welcomed there as an honoured guest, but has in fact assisted with some of the services provided. So, in a sense, Broadmoor is his alma mater. I must ask him some time why he liked it so much.

I had equipped myself with a bottle of sherry, but was compelled to leave it in the car as we were subjected to a ludicrous degree of searching on the way into Broadmoor. I drank some of it gratefully on the way back.

Thursday April 23, 1998

Visited Brian Vale for the last time at the Scrubs. He is very pleased to be moving to Grendon next week. I hope to visit him there, but he wishes to settle in first.

Friday April 24, 1998

Visited Father Fred at Wandsworth. Last week the *Sunday Telegraph* had run a prominent story headed, 'Longford Helps a Paedophile to Jump NHS Queue'. It arose from my having written to the hospital about Father Fred's hernia and his obtaining an operation not long afterwards. It ignored the fact that he had been waiting for such an operation for three years.

What was more surprising was that it quoted verbatim a letter I had written to him. It ran as follows: 'I enclose a letter just received [from the hospital]. I hope that it is encouraging. You have had to bear so much. I am looking forward to seeing you on Friday.'

I had telephoned the author of the article, the health correspondent of the *Sunday Telegraph*, and assured her that I did not feel damaged myself. In fact I was flattered by the suggestion that I actually help prisoners when I visit them.

She seemed relieved as she assured me that she is a great admirer of mine.

I could not, however, answer for Father Fred. There might be repercussions from the quotation of my letter to him. I think she realised that this was, to say the least, open to criticism. It was against any rules known to me.

When I saw Father Fred he told me that he had already written to the Press Complaints Commission to make sure that his complaint was not put aside as out of time which happened to him once before.

I am a little torn here. I don't want to make a fuss about my treatment, but it may be that any legal complaint about the use of my letter would have to start with me. I have spoken to Andrew McCooey and will be letting him have at least the *Sunday Telegraph* article.

Incidentally, Father Fred tells me that he is very popular with the other prisoners. It must be remembered that he is the outstanding figure in the vulnerable wing whose residents are, to say the least, by no means popular with the rest of the inmates.

Friday May 1, 1998

Visited Ray Masterman in Belmarsh Prison near Woolwich. He seems to have accepted the decision to extradite him back to America and to be anxious to get back there as quickly as possible to begin fighting his appeal. What worries him most, very understandably, is the position of his wife and three children, who are at the moment homeless.

His wife, whom I have learnt to know and respect, seems determined to follow him back to America. They seem to assume that the three children, the eldest nineteen, will be able to look after themselves if they can find a flat. It sounds perilous to me, but I have much confidence in his wife.

Sunday May 24, 1998

This last week has been a sad wash-out in my own case. Walking back from visiting Matt Oliver last Sunday, I tripped over a kerb and was picked up unconscious. I was taken to hospital and though I was allowed home next day I have been in a battered condition ever since.

Sunday June 7, 1998

I have resumed my diary after a fortnight's break. I am slowly recovering.

Visited Father Fred at Wandsworth on Wednesday. Found him in his full ebullient form. He is very pleased that, partly due to my intervention, he is getting his hour's exercise and, according to himself, he is out-pacing colleagues. He still has three operations in front of him.

Wednesday June 10, 1998

Another visit to Philip Portington and Lee McGregor at Wandsworth. Everything in Philip's life is suspended while we await the decision of the European Court on June 24. Neither he nor I seem to be sure what will follow if the case is won that day. I gather that the trial would then be held to have been unfair, but that automatic release would certainly not follow.

What an extraordinary life Philip has had. He left school at fifteen and joined the Foreign Legion, altering his age to eighteen. He served five years in the Foreign Legion in Vietnam and all sorts of exciting places. He has a hell of a life story to tell and I gather is writing it with the help of a lady novelist who visited him several times in Greece.

Lee McGregor looks quite cheerful, but in my eyes is one of the loneliest prisoners I have known. It is a little hard to understand his circumstances. He tells me that he has no family or friends to visit him, but I am not quite sure if I have got that right. He is in his cell twenty-four hours a day except, I think, for meals.

His sentence of eleven years has been increased to a life sentence by the Appeal Court, which he did not even know was considering the case.

After my last visit I approached the chief medical officer at Wandsworth and obtained the idea that his psychiatric condition was being taken seriously. But now that does not seem to be the case.

I have therefore written to the Minister for Prisons, Joyce Quinn, asking for her personal attention. Lee is a schizophrenic. I now discover he is a diabetic. He is genuinely fearful of what he might do if released from prison. Since I last saw him he was involved in an argument about football with a fellow prisoner on the exercise ground and finished up by seizing him by the throat. He can't remember why, but luckily released him before doing any damage.

He is now in the prison hospital, but has not been seen by a doctor. I am sure that I have done the right thing in taking up Lee's future at a ministerial level.

Monday June 15, 1998

Garter Day. Cannot resist mentioning my experience at Windsor Castle this year. I sat between the Queen and Princess Anne. Elizabeth, author of half a dozen books on royalty, was ideally placed between Prince Charles and Prince Philip. I had sat next to the Queen twenty-seven years earlier as the newest Garter knight and had shaken hands with her every year as she passed by before the lunch.

But this time I felt I began to know her for the first time. Prince Charles was sitting opposite. She allowed me to raise all the obvious questions. Her replies in some cases must be treated as confidential, but I had the overwhelming sense that this was not a monarch talking about a successor, but a fond mother talking with her eyes open about her son.

Wednesday June 24, 1998

Roy motored me down to Whitemoor to visit Des Nilsen. Roy had taken the initiative in writing to Des a rather brilliant letter which drew a rather brilliant reply. Roy had a kind of excuse in setting out to reassure Des about the state of my health. But it was fairly obvious to me, and I welcomed it, that he was anxious to promote a relationship.

Des in his reply made a couple of jokes which would seem rather bold in writing to a complete stranger. He said, 'Frank may know the Queen but I know a lot of "queens".' And later, 'Frank may be an old peer but I am an old queer.'

When I saw Des I repeated these jokes with appreciation. He asked me whether Roy was of the same disposition as himself – what is now called gay. I had always assumed that he guessed as much when he made the jokes just quoted.

Later I told Roy of the conversation. He considered that I had made a gross error and had insulted him. However, since then Roy has had a second letter from Nilsen (he had written to him a second time) referring to my visit. So all seems to be well on that front, though Roy, as he will admit, is a man of moods.

Friday June 26, 1998

Unusually, visited three prisoners in one morning at Wandsworth. Father Fred had written urgently, wanting to see me. In the event I spent a large part of the time with him.

He was understandably very annoyed at getting a very

bad report from the sex-education psychologist. I have yet to see it and when I do I am going to take up the matter with the governor and, if necessary, the minister. According to Father Fred, they have derided his religion, treating him as a self-appointed bishop, and in effect accused him of not repenting of his crimes. I will report further when I have seen their report.

Father Fred is full of fun and I am sure teased these three psychologists to the point where they have sought their revenge. They seem to have admitted that he was cleverer than they were, but this seems to have turned them against him. I suppose that if he made fools of them in front of the class, it is understandable if intolerable.

My next visit was to Philip Portington. Since I last saw him, the Strasbourg court has heard submissions. The news appeared to be good, but nothing will be known for certain for perhaps another fortnight when the judgment is received. At that point it seems likely that I shall be called on to write to the Greek government and perhaps the Home Secretary. However, so far so good.

A rather hurried visit to Lee McGregor, my schizophrenic young friend, whose eleven-year sentence was recently increased to life. I am sure that he is right in begging the authorities to transfer him to Broadmoor.

Wednesday July 8, 1998

Visited Wandsworth. Another interesting talk with the unfortunate Lee McGregor. Since I saw him last I have been told by the Minister for Prisons that he has been examined twice by visiting psychiatrists and not found mentally ill. I had understood from him that he was a schizophrenic.

Lee asked me to verify this from Dr Chesterman, psychiatrist at the Maudsley Hospital. I have since been on to

Dr Chesterman who told me that Lee was diagnosed as suffering from a personality disorder. Dr Chesterman is going to send me a report of his to this effect. Whatever the medical experts say, I am utterly convinced that Lee ought to be in hospital rather than prison and shall keep on working towards that end.

Wednesday July 22, 1998

A very successful visit by Elizabeth and me to Myra. We spent about an hour and a half with her at her explicit request. I would have visited her several times in the last few years, but she had apparently feared the publicity.

Whatever the reason, nothing could have been warmer than her reception. Elizabeth, who had visited her twice before, but many years ago, and Myra fell into each other's arms which created a terrific atmosphere. Myra and I, if left to ourselves, might have become too argumentative. I told her that I had written an article about her and wanted to have her permission to publish it. She opposed the idea. Her solicitor had been urging her that there should be no publicity until after her next court case in October.

In the end I persuaded her to agree, in principle, that if she liked the article I could get it published in a reputable paper. She accepted *The Times* as such, although owned by Murdoch and associated in her mind with the venomous assaults in *The Sun*.

She was happier than I ever remember her. She has a room, not a cell, and a piece of garden to herself. More importantly, she has found an inner peace through her religion. I was surprised to learn that Mass was not available in the prison although there was frequent communion. There was no Catholic chaplain, but she was obtaining much spiritual comfort from a deacon.

She asked us for flowers for her birthday which was to occur the following day. We managed to get them to her on her birthday through the amazingly efficient Interflora. I am still trying to produce the right kind of wristwatch for her.

Wednesday September 9, 1998

Another visit to Father Fred. Quite a lot to talk about, apart from religious discussion. Incidentally, he mentioned that he was a professor of theology at the age of seventeen. I told him that I would believe anything he told me, but this one was a hard one to stomach. He assured me that, in a theological college, at seventeen he was made a professor teaching students. I said, as an old university don who never made the professorial grade, that I looked up to him all the more, but still found it difficult to believe that being a professor at that college was what I understood by a professor.

He has asked me to take up a complicated issue with a local authority which has adversely affected one of the properties of the Old Catholic order. This I shall do, though I keep telling him that he somewhat overestimates my influence. More importantly, I have received a long letter from the Home Office minister, Gareth Williams (Lord Williams of Mostyn), in reply to one of mine about Father Fred. Father Fred feels strongly, and I am sure rightly, that the report of the psychologists in charge of his sex-offenders' course was grossly unfair to him. Gareth Williams insists that there is nothing to be done about it except lay all the issues before the Parole Board. We are now making plans to see how that can best be done.

To give a sample of Father Fred's religious knowledge, the night before I saw him I attended Mass. The priest read the gospel for the day which came from the first chapter of

St Matthew, tracing the genealogy of Christ and the immediate events leading to his birth. I was puzzled at the time by the emphasis laid on the descent from Abraham through Joseph who was, after all, not his real father at all.

I asked a very well-qualified priest on the way whether anything was known of Mary's family background (it was Mary's Day). He and another priest who was there could not produce on the spur of the moment, but Father Fred at once pointed out that you could trace her through her cousin Elizabeth and in that way work back to Abraham. Not a usual piece of learning picked up from a prisoner.

Wednesday October 28, 1998

Thelma Cross, my constant friend for over thirty years in the House of Lords, drove me to Whitemoor (two and a quarter hours) and back to Westminster (three hours). I was visiting Des Nilsen after the usual six week or so interval. Des was much the same as ever, but an hour and a half passed happily which I think was partly due to Thelma's presence. Des, as all are aware, is a homosexual, but like many other homosexuals he is capable of taking a liking to a woman. He was obviously pleased to see Thelma again and to have a little audience. It enabled him to tease me without being offensive.

He told me that the issue of his autobiography will shortly be coming before the court. I did not gather that there was anything I could do about it, at any rate at the moment.

He has written 700 pages. His editor is expecting to cut it to half that length and show Des the result, but although he tells me that the book was not smuggled out, the authorities are refusing to let him see the revised version and sign a contract. So the struggle continues.

We talked once again about his homosexuality and how it had affected his life. The fact of concealing it for so long (twelve years in the army) seems to have produced a kind of secret war between himself and society which led to terrible results.

It is now sixteen years since he began his prison term. He seems to have conquered the strange feelings that led to the tragedies. I very much hope that that is so. I asked him whether he was creating anything (literary or musical). He said, 'I am relaxing, reading Orwell at the moment.' But he later disclosed that he was writing poetry. The creative urge is evidently still alive.

Friday October 30, 1998

Visited Lee McGregor again in Wandsworth. He tells me that he is likely to be moved at the beginning of November, I hope to Brixton. What matters above all is that he should receive treatment, or at any rate mental care of some kind, which is not possible for him in Wandsworth for the odd reason that he is a life prisoner.

Wednesday November 4, 1998

Visited the familiar Wandsworth to meet a prisoner whose mother I had encountered on an earlier visit there who said that her son would like to see me. He is twenty-five, educated at St Edward's School, Oxford, but obviously still trying to find his vocation.

At the time of his arrest he was employed in a nightclub and was convicted of selling drugs to an undercover policeman. He is serving a three-year sentence, but hopes that in practice it will be no more than a year. He is to be 'tagged' for the last six months.

He is good-looking and agreeable. He expects to be moved shortly to the male prison at High Point, Suffolk; Myra is at the female one across the road. I met his fiancée, as I hope she is, with his mother at the encounter mentioned earlier. I hope and believe that it could be a happy and satisfactory marriage.

Unfortunately a very reliable driver misunderstood the day and I was half an hour late reaching the prison. This meant that I could not see Father Fred and left word with the officer in charge explaining the circumstances. I ventured to add, 'I hope that you will tell him politely.' He replied a little testily, 'We officers are always polite.'

Thursday November 5, 1998

The Appeal Court has ruled on the Home Office decision that Myra should stay in prison for all her life. When I arrived at court I was not surprised to find a lot of media men and women who asked me what I thought her chances were. I replied fifty-fifty. But meeting Edward Fitzgerald, her counsel, on the way in I was warned that I was too sanguine.

In the event Lord Woolf, speaking for the Appeal Court, rejected her application saying that the reasons were set out in a document available.

The journalists in the court asked me for an immediate reaction. I expressed deep disappointment but Edward, whom I met on the way out, told me that things were far from hopeless. In the first place, appeal to the House of Lords has been granted which he told me was far from automatic. Moreover the document, which runs into many pages, contains a passage which I have yet to study properly in which Woolf indicates that he would not have rejected her case if it meant that Myra must necessarily stay in prison for life. In other words there is a loophole, as indeed there was in the earlier judicial review.

I must look more carefully into the phrasing of the judgment. There is a reference to the need for maintaining public confidence in the system, which has a nasty air about it.

There are further grounds for a small degree of optimism in signs of a slightly improved attitude by Jack Straw himself. As already recorded, he has welcomed the All-Party Home Affairs' Committee's recommendation that more use should be made of alternatives to prison.

Meanwhile Elizabeth and I will be visiting Myra later this month. David Astor saw her more recently than I did and confirms my sense that she was happier than one can remember. I hope and believe that her strong religious convictions carry her through this new unwelcome development.

Saturday November 7, 1998

Received a distressed letter from Father Fred telling me that he had been transferred to Winchester, but also that he had been told I did not want to see him. When I meet this kind of discourtesy in prisons I have to remind myself that I would not be able to be a prison officer.

He complained of the bullying received at Wandsworth, but seems nevertheless very unhappy at the transfer. I was glad to hear that he is in the prison hospital in Winchester. There is no doubt that he needs a lot of medical attention.

Wednesday November 11, 1998

Visited Father Fred, this time at Winchester Prison. The warmth of my welcome was quite surprising. A principal officer took me to a private office and provided coffee without charge. This compared favourably with Wandsworth, where the charge is fifty pence a cup. The atmosphere was so friendly that I suggested at the end I should write to the governor to thank him for the kind arrangements. Father

Fred welcomed the idea and so did the principal officer who was happy to have his name mentioned.

I have never received quite this treatment when visiting an individual prisoner, though I have, of course, been a guest of governors on various occasions.

Friday November 13, 1998

Visited Lee McGregor at Wandsworth again. I have rather revised my opinion that he is a mental case and ought to be in hospital. I think that it is better for him not to think of himself as mad if he can be treated in prison. This seems possible if he is transferred as planned to Brixton where a number of courses are available. At Wandsworth he was not eligible for any such because he is serving a life sentence.

To my complete surprise he told me that about a year ago he won a prize in a competition for knowledge of St Mark's Gospel. I discovered after a few minutes' discussion that he was quite well-versed in that gospel.

His trouble, mental or otherwise, is that he suddenly loses his temper. He sounds the ideal subject for a course in anger control.

Wednesday November 25, 1998

Elizabeth and I visited Myra. She suffers from various disabilities, including a gammy leg, though she moved about without her stick. I cannot believe that any honest person, meeting her now, would fail to recognise her as a remarkable woman.

She has drawn considerable encouragement from various passages of the long judgment of the Court of Appeal which rejects her case at that stage, but allows her to appeal to the Lords.

The essential fact about her now is that she has become a deeply religious woman and, as she told us on the last occasion, is as happy as she could expect to be in prison. She handed me as I left what she called her 'credo'. It is about the same length as that used in Catholic churches. I should emphasise that she is a devout Catholic, as priest after priest has testified.

She is, I am bound to say, a little contradictory in one respect. She does not want to seem to be promoting propaganda on her behalf. She prefers to leave it to the brilliant legal team led by Edward Fitzgerald, my grandson-in-law. But she was, it seems, happy enough for me to secure publication for her credo. I duly approached *The Catholic Herald* who intend to publish it in their next issue. Joe Jenkins, the deputy editor, looked up the eighth-century monk whose name was attached to it and found that he was a Buddhist. There was certainly nothing which Christians would find unwelcome.

I should add that Elizabeth and she embraced each other before and after the visit in the warmest possible manner. She makes it plain that she prefers a visit from both of us. She prefers to see me as her dad rather than her senile boyfriend.

Thursday November 26, 1998

Joined others at the Cambridge Union in resisting the motion reducing the age of consent for men and women to fourteen. We won fairly comfortably. I was told that if the figure had been sixteen instead of fourteen we should have been well beaten.

Friday November 27, 1998

Visited Lee McGregor, now in Brixton. He definitely prefers it to Wandsworth, being out of his cell for at least half the day.

He is attending an English class and also hopes to attend a Bible-study discussion group.

I came away still very uncertain about the right venue for him, but more hopeful than on past occasions.

Wednesday December 9, 1998

Visited Lee McGregor in Brixton once more. I had booked the visit. When I got there, I was not expected.

There is a Brixton telephone number for legal visits, but one can never get through. One therefore rings the duty governor or such like, and makes the appointment, but somehow it gets lost.

Lee is having, relatively speaking, a wonderful time – two classes a week on education, one on jazz, one on computers, plus a Bible-study group. He is grateful to me for my supposed influence in bringing this about. I doubt whether I deserve the credit.

Monday December 14, 1998

Asked a question in the House of Lords about the expressed views of the Lord Chief Justice on the treatment of life prisoners. He had said, more than once, that their sentencing should be removed from the Home Office and transferred to the judiciary.

The simple solution would be in fact to place mandatory life prisoners on the same footing as discretionary life prisoners. In the latter case the decisions of the Parole Board are final.

Wrapped up with this issue is another one – whether imprisonment for life should ever mean exactly that, removing all hope for a prisoner. The answer I received from the ever-astute Gareth Williams, former chairman of the Bar

Council, now a Minister for Prisons and Deputy Leader of the House, was evasive but negative. I got in a final word after the short discussion, accusing him of 'ducking' the issue.

In my question I pointed out that the Home Secretary is very likely to be influenced by the tabloid press. I had, of course, Myra in mind. But, there again, the minister was evasive. There is no doubt that he is not only a very clever lawyer, but has a parliamentary style which the house finds very agreeable.

Tuesday December 15, 1998

A fellow peer asked me after my question on Monday whether I would support him when today he asked his question about prison education. I duly did so, recalling yet again the shocking fact that the prison education budget was actually cut by the last government in spite of the rapid increase of prisoners and that, until recently, the Labour government seemed to be continuing the process.

Gareth Williams disclosed what I had not been able to obtain by my own enquiries, namely that there was now going to be an increase in this budget. How that relates to the rapid increase in the prison population in recent years needs further exploration, as indeed does the question of whether the increase in this same population has at last been halted.

Wednesday December 16, 1998

During the week the welcome news was published that the House of Lords' decision against General Pinochet was overturned by a further Lords' judgment. Lord Hoffman, one of the five who heard the case, was revealed as having been deeply involved with Amnesty International, who were active in demanding extradition. So, it seemed at the cost of

£500,000, the case should be tried again.

I am much drawn to the idea of interviewing General Pinochet, if at all possible. I would find no difficulty in repeating what I have said elsewhere, that he ought to be sent back to Chile forthwith. In an interview, however, I would need to discuss his record in Chile and, at present, I am too ignorant of it to do the job properly. I am thinking of ways to become better informed.

Thursday December 24, 1998

A long-deferred visit to Eddie Richardson, my friend, as he reminded me, of thirty years. An old professional boxer, he looked extremely fit. He tells me that he is allowed to do painting of some kind, but is still denied the use of oils.

Long Lartin is supposed to be a top-security prison. I had taken the precaution of arriving early, so got in without the difficulties experienced on previous occasions. But I was not even allowed to leave a Christmas card, let alone a present of a paperback. No one can be discovered to defend these arrangements, which are, in fact, indefensible.

Eddie is still on category A, which means that he cannot ever have any real chance of parole. He is going to let me know how to take the matter up further, which I shall do with enthusiasm.

Thursday December 31, 1998

Another visit to Lee McGregor whose gratitude to me is moving. He is, undoubtedly, receiving a great deal of useful education and thoroughly appreciates the fact. He was worried that by the time he left Brixton he would not have had time to undertake the psychology courses (anger control) which he understood were necessary if he was to get parole.

After making contact with the Parole Board I was able to reassure him. The only thing that worries him at the moment is that he is not getting the special food for diabetics which he has received in earlier prisons and indeed Brixton when he was there before. I have spoken to one of the medical officers and am writing to the governor about it.

Tuesday January 12, 1999

Initiated a one and a half hour debate in the Lords. I asked the government what steps they are taking to reflect the recommendations of the All-Party Home Affairs' Committee which has called for a major switch from imprisonment to the use of alternative remedies.

The government has welcomed that report, but what are they doing about it? Gareth Williams, the very astute Minister for Prisons, mentioned a number of steps they would take. He could point to a slight fall in the prison population recently, but was chary about forecasting the future.

I would have been less surprised at this if I had been aware that earlier in the afternoon the Home Secretary had announced a policy of 'three burglaries and you get three years in prison'. This apparently will increase the prison population by 4,000. So the whole matter is wrapped in doubt as before.

Wednesday January 13, 1999

Another visit to Lee McGregor at Brixton. I was delighted to hear that the wing governor had called on him the day before, having received the complaint that he was not getting the food required to cope with his diabetes. The governor had immediately put the matter right and he was now receiving this form of medication. I would like to think that a letter from me to the governor was responsible, but the matter had also been taken up by the prison officer assigned to Lee. I would be happy to think that he was responsible.

I was a little bit shocked, perhaps more surprised than shocked, by a conversation with the prison officer in charge of the visiting wing. I do not think he knew Lee McGregor personally. I thought that I was saying something very acceptable when I congratulated him on the treatment being accorded Lee. I said, 'I think that it is rather wonderful that he should be going to half a dozen educational classes a week.' The officer is not a grumpy man, but he replied grumpily, 'I wish my children could have such good treatment.' I was left wondering how many prison officers feel envious of prisoners.

On the way out I ran into a party of four young women visitors. One of them said to me, 'Could you please remind me of your name?' I said, 'I'll tell you mine if you tell me yours.' She said, 'I'm Madeleine.' I said, 'I'm Frank.' She said, 'Oh yes. You're the one campaigning for Myra Hindley.' I said, 'I hope you agree with me.' She said, 'Very much so.'

That incident came in useful that afternoon when I addressed the sixth form at the Francis Holland Girls' School in west London. I was told that the girls were especially interested in Myra Hindley. I therefore started off with her before dealing with penal matters. The girls seemed very favourable to her.

Thursday January 14, 1999

Tony Blair addressed the Labour peers. Ted Graham, chairman of the latter, had kindly invited me as the senior Labour peer to ask the first question. I decided to ask, 'Is some redistribution of wealth from rich to poor still part of the New Labour ideal?'

I gave the Prime Minister's office some advance notice of the question. I did not wish to catch him unawares.

In the event he rattled off a long answer touching on many points, mentioning redistribution as he swept along, but leaving the audience no wiser about the government's reply to my question. I have said in his favour elsewhere that he left on me, and no doubt on others, the impression of being a really good man. New Labour seems to most of us old-timers a different party from the one we joined.

I was congratulated by several of my colleagues on 'asking a question on behalf of us all'. I was particularly pleased that one of those congratulating me was an elegant young peeress whose name (not her telephone number) I made a note to find out. I am happy, for the moment at least, with my new assessment of New Labour. It is not the same as Old Labour, but a little child of Old Labour. That is to say, one of its parents is Old Labour. The other is Tony Blair himself.

Friday January 15, 1999

After a conversation with William Oddie, my boss at *The Catholic Herald*, I dictated to Maggie in the House of Lords my column for next week's issue. She faxed it to the editor who at once rang and told me on the telephone how much he liked it. It was headed by me, 'If Mandy, why not Robin?' In the light of the troubles of Peter Mandelson and Robin Cook, I raised the whole question of whether sexual misbehaviour disqualifies a man for high office. I argued that in the case of a minister, most obviously a Foreign Secretary or, of course, Prime Minister, you cannot divorce his private from his public life. I concluded by saying that if a man sets out to lead the people they are entitled to know the truth about him, warts and all.

Thursday January 21, 1999

I received a very welcome letter from the Prime Minister offering me a life peerage, to enable me to continue to sit in the Lords after hereditary peers' voting rights are abolished. Many people assume that I have a life peerage already, but I was made a peer in 1945 and life peerages were not introduced until 1958. Later, in 1961, I inherited my brother's title on his death.

I was hoping that somehow or other I would survive the reform, but it is much easier for me to play a full part in discussing and, if necessary, criticising the government's proposals now that my own future is assured. I am busying myself at the moment with suggesting to the authorities the names of at least half a dozen Labour hereditary peers who should be given life peerages.

Yesterday Margaret Jay, Leader of the House, had read out a statement also being made by the Prime Minister in the Commons. I admired the sang-froid and good nature with which she told the massed hereditaries they were for 'the chop', and the careful way she answered the questions. I myself asked a question which would ensure my popularity where it matters: 'Some of us who have been here a long time are concerned about the future of the staff. Can the government promise that, in any reforms, much reducing the number of members of the House, their interests will be fully considered?' Margaret gave an inconclusive reply, but when I spoke to Black Rod, a senior Lord's official, afterwards he seemed fairly happy.

Friday January 22, 1999

Jonathan Aitken's mother came to lunch with me on Friday, just as her son's fate is on the front page of every newspaper.

She is an amazing woman, aged, we are told, eighty-eight, but looking twenty years or more younger. Very upright in every sense, no sign of a stick.

I knew her father, Lord Rugby, quite well when he was the British representative in Dublin during the Second World War. He had previously been Head of the Colonial Service. We played golf together at Portmanock. He was the finest type of Englishman, and looked the part.

I cannot begin to describe Jonathan here. There are three sides to his character. First, a brilliant politician and member of the Cabinet until he resigned three years ago. Second, a man who often lived too dangerously – with women, in Middle East finance, and with the law courts. Third, a man who has been a believing Christian since his boyhood, but is now exhibiting a kind of Christian heroism facing the near certainty, as he sees it, of prison with edifying courage. If that happens I am sure that he will eventually emerge and will fully redeem himself with fine service to the community.

Wednesday January 27, 1999

Visited my friend Lee McGregor once more, and a prisoner who has written to me called Spencer Trott.

I had a brief interview with the latter. He was being visited at the same time by someone from the London Lighthouse, an organisation which is concerned with sufferers from AIDS. About six years ago Spencer was sentenced to six years in prison for buggery. He was allowed out on licence towards the end of the period, but was then charged with assault, for which he is awaiting trial.

He wants me to back him up in his appeal against the conviction for buggery. I felt bound to tell him that I doubted whether I could be useful, but would be glad to get in touch with his solicitor. I look forward to seeing him next time I visit Brixton.

He was quite tall but not powerfully built. I made a feeble joke about needing the protection of the Lighthouse man if he got violent. He insisted that the victim of his assault had suggested intercourse, but afterwards turned nasty. I leave it there for the moment.

Thursday February 4, 1999

Paid my fortnightly visit to Father Fred. I had a little more difficulty than usual in getting in because the friendly deputy governor was on leave, but as usual I was escorted into an office.

The news from Father Fred is, I suppose, the worst since I have been visiting him. He has been physically attacked by what sounds like a crazy prisoner, who banged him on the head more than once. The prisoner was, I gather, some kind of informer, who was, therefore, in the vulnerable wing along with the sex offenders.

The prisoner was moved but another prisoner remained who continued the attacks. Poor Father Fred's eyesight has now been affected. He has written me a long letter of complaint to the governor which I shall be forwarding with my support.

It is particularly sad because I was beginning to say that Winchester was the best prison I had ever visited. But alas! with prisons you can never be certain of anything. I am also waiting to do two other things: (1) to write to the Parole Board about Father Fred's fine qualities; and (2) to ask the governor whether he ought to be moved to another prison in order to undertake courses, for example, sex-education courses, which are not available in Winchester.

Wednesday February 10, 1999

Visited three prisoners in Brixton. The first, Spencer Trott, I had only seen for a few minutes on the last occasion. An agreeable, young-looking 37-year-old, he is a lifelong homosexual.

He has a strange story. He is anxious for me to help in his appeal against a six-year sentence for buggery.

The alleged offence took place when he was still serving time for a previous offence. He insists that his cell-mate encouraged him to masturbate, but that no buggery resulted.

I don't hold out much hope of being really useful to him, except that I feel that while he remains in prison he may enjoy my visits.

Next came Philip Portington. For once my visit would clear up a misunderstanding. He was convicted fourteen years ago of murdering a stranger he gave a lift to when on holiday in Greece. Andrew McCooey visited him more than once in Greece and has tried to help him ever since.

Andrew told me before I saw Portington this time that he had now changed his plea and admitted self-defence which may have led to the man's death. Portington himself, however, insists that he has not changed his plea. He has simply said that he is ready to accept responsibility in the sense that the lift he gave the victim led to his being murdered by someone else. So I must leave Andrew and him to work it out.

He raised, however, a wider issue. He says that it is generally understood that to obtain parole at a reasonable time, one has to admit guilt. I am pursuing this question. My daughter Rachel told me that prisoners seem to believe this, but that it is denied by the authorities. Certainly it is worth looking into.

Lee McGregor next. I have become very fond of Lee. It really does seem that he has turned over a new leaf. He is now attending half a dozen courses and waiting to hear from a barrister who is hoping to organise an appeal for him on the grounds that his violent rages were due to misunderstood diabetes. The barrister wishes Lee to authorise talks between me and the barrister. I am awaiting further news.

Thursday February 11, 1999

Visited Des Nilsen at Whitemoor. Motored down by my former secretary and friend for many years, Thelma Cross. On three previous occasions she has been allowed into the prison with me in my meetings with Des. This time, in spite of a good deal of insistence beforehand, they refused her entry. I was told that, as he was category A, it had to be authorised in the first place by him.

At the end of my session with Des I said to the prison officer who was escorting him away that I wanted to help Des, but he doesn't want me to help him. Des gave me one of his sardonic smiles.

It all comes back to the conversation I reported earlier when I said to him, 'You're rather arrogant, aren't you, Des?' and he said, 'You'd be arrogant if you were regarded by everyone as a monster and were spending your life in prison. I've got to be what you call arrogant to survive.' In other words he does value my help, but doesn't like to seem to be pleading for it.

Two immediate issues concern him: his memoirs and his poems. His memoirs have been edited by a friend and are being considered by a publisher. He wants me to talk to other publishers, but there is not very much point in this until I know whether the present publisher is going to take the book.

Secondly, his poems: he has written enough I gather to make a short book. But the Home Office says that he must not publish them because he must not conduct business from prison. He seems to have a very strong case here, which I will actively pursue.

Wednesday February 17, 1999

Took part in a debate on the place of the judiciary in the House of Lords. The discussions mainly centred on the double role of the Lord Chancellor, as a politician and a judge, and the place of the Law Lords who might be speaking in the House on matters overlapping their judicial functions. I took the opportunity, however, to submit that the judiciary, headed by the Law Lords, was an essential bulwark against mob rule and, in particular, the menace of the tabloids. I concentrated on the story of the continued persecution of Myra by the tabloids.

The Sun has always been particularly vicious, but recently the *The Mirror* has joined in. It dredged up a story of Myra and a lady friend being left alone for a short while in Cookham Wood Prison four years ago with an eight-year-old child.

Thursday February 18, 1999

Another visit to Father Fred. I was glad to hear that both the prisoners who had attacked him have been moved. He has been left with pains in the head and some eye trouble, which I gather is being tackled. The sad news is that the deputy governor, who has always received me and taken me to a governor's office for a meeting with 'Fred', is retiring.

Wednesday February 24, 1999

Set out to make three visits at Brixton. A very encouraging talk with Lee McGregor. His treatment in Brixton shows the

Prison Service at its best. On the morning I saw him, he had woken up feeling very unwell. To steady himself he gripped the railing and was told by a prison officer to stop holding it. He replied in his own version to me – 'F-- off' – which would certainly have normally landed him in the punishment block. The prison officer, however, at once realised he was unwell. A doctor was summoned. It was discovered that his blood count was much too low. He was given the necessary medication. Full marks to a much-criticised Prison Service.

Then I saw Spencer Trott again. I have failed to make contact with London Lighthouse, the organisation which helps people with HIV and AIDS, and which he feels might help him.

I was also booked to see Philip Portington. However, I got the message that he did not wish to see me. I was given no reason, so I must take it that he does not feel that I can be useful to him.

This led me on to a wider enquiry. Are prisoners told of intended visits and is their consent and availability secured before a visit is booked? The answer in Brixton is, 'No.' I am taking up the matter with the governor. I always avoid going to a prison unless I know that the prisoner is available and wants to see me.

Monday March 1, 1999

Called, by appointment, on Philip Wheatley, a leading official in the Prison Service, chairman of the category A committee. Eddie Richardson had suggested that Wheatley was the one man whom I should see in the effort to get him removed from category A.

While on category A it seems that it is unlikely that he would ever get parole, although he has now served eleven years in prison for drug dealing. His record in prison is impeccable. Moreover, uniquely in my experience, he has become a successful artist, never having painted previously. He has won a succession of Koestler Awards.

Wheatley was franker than I had expected. He told me that on the last occasion Eddie's case had come up, he had still been regarded as presenting a risk on release. This was for three reasons. (1) He consorted in prison with professional criminals; (2) he had not shown any real remorse for his crimes; and (3) he was believed to possess criminal associations outside.

I told Wheatley that this all seemed to be very unreasonable. It is difficult to see how a long-term prisoner could fail to associate with others in the same boat. He had, moreover, attended an offender course in the way required.

Thursday March 11, 1999

Visited once more Medway Training Centre in Kent, subject of a damning report in January, with a view to a speech in the House of Lords next week. The centre is financed and run by Group 4. The contract had been signed by the last government and taken over by the present one.

The young people (mixed in theory, but nearly all boys) go there between the ages of twelve and fourteen and stay no more than a year, often much less. The staff number one hundred, the young people twenty-nine. On the face of it, an indefensible ratio but I must study comparable ratios in children's homes and local government secure units. The deputy director of the Howard League had told me beforehand that they – and, she believed, the other penal reform bodies – were opposed to the whole thing. She said that the young people should go to the local government secure units. I was told at the centre that such places were often reluctant to take the youngsters and apparently could not be coerced. I must look into this further.

I was exceptionally lucky in being welcomed and looked after by the officer from Group 4 primarily responsible for the centre. He had been a probation officer and a health inspector who had also worked for the Home Office, personally advis-ing the Home Secretary. No one could deny his knowledge of the various attempts made to cope with misbehaving boys and girls.

He showed his wisdom by inviting a young inmate to join me when I was having lunch. Aged just fifteen he told me he had committed a hundred burglaries and had been given many kinds of sentence without going to prison.

But he was only spending three months and three weeks in the centre and then being sent back from Kent to Nottingham with no clear idea at all of his own future. It would hardly have been possible to produce a better illustration of the pointlessness of the centre, in spite of the evident high-mindedness of those running it. No one could seriously argue that in these few months his approach to life would be altered, that he would give up being a young criminal.

The reason for sending him to the centre seemed to be that it would be a tougher punishment than any he had yet received. But against that it was explained to me that the centre was in practice no kind of prison, but the best sort of children's home.

Wednesday March 24, 1999

Received a message that Lee McGregor did not wish to see me as planned. On my previous visit to Brixton I received that same message about Philip Portington, learning later that in fact he was tied up with the Samaritans.

In my experience, prisoners whom I have been visiting

have three reasons for not wishing to see me on a particular occasion: they are not well, I have offended them, or they are tied up elsewhere.

It was particularly surprising in Lee's case, because he had expressed himself as being so grateful for what I have tried to do for him hitherto. I complained a little while ago to the governor of Brixton that in that prison, unlike others, no attempt is made to discover whether the inmate wishes to see a particular visitor on a particular occasion. That issue is still apparently being looked into. I shall be very sorry indeed if Lee does not want to see me in future.

Wednesday April 7, 1999

Visited Des Nilsen at Whitemoor. An unusual experience. After travelling for several hours from Chelsea I was slightly disconcerted to be told Nilsen didn't wish to see me. I asked to see an officer, but by the time he arrived the news was different. Des now did wish to see me.

Des explained that when the first batch went over to meet visitors he was told that I was not there and so abandoned the project. It is just possible that I hadn't arrived by then. But I am left consoling myself with the reflection that prison is not like anywhere else.

This is the third time recently I have been told a prisoner does not want to see me. Is it just a coincidence? Is it possible that I am an unwelcome visitor? It would not amaze me if this were true or put me off my visits. Prisons probably reckon that a visit from me produces a criticism of their arrangements. Sometimes they welcome these. For example, in Brixton they are now aware of the difficulty of reaching them on the telephone. More often perhaps they don't. As I say, the show goes on.

Thursday April 8, 1999

Visited Lee McGregor at Brixton. I am afraid that the news of a possible appeal in his case is not good. He is, as will be recalled, doing a life sentence for attempted murder and rape. He remembers nothing because he had been drinking so heavily. His appeal would be based on the fact that his sudden rages spring from his diabetes, but, rightly or wrongly, his appeal seems unlikely to go forward.

Wednesday April 14, 1999

Another visit to Father Fred at Winchester. One of the young men who earlier attacked him physically is now coming to him for guidance.

Wednesday May 5, 1999

Visited Lee McGregor again at Wandsworth. He told me a sad story about his mother whom I had welcomed at the House of Lords not long ago. She had fainted while waiting to see him and in her fall broke her ankle in two places. She is now in hospital without having seen him. I promised to call on her at St Thomas's, which is nice and close to the House of Lords.

I spoke to her by telephone and found her delighted to see me, but when the time came I was told that she was not well enough. I rang her later and spoke to her and found her still uncertain whether she would be well enough to return in the next day or two to Newcastle. I am going to make contact again this week.

I was glad to see Philip Portington again. He is very unhappy that he is still in Brixton. He insists that he will have to go to an open prison before he is finally released. Andrew

McCooey is now going to draft a letter for me to the Minister for Prisons in pursuit of his cause.

Wednesday May 19, 1999

Visited Des Nilson again at Whitemoor. I am determined to help Des to get his poems published somehow or other. By legal means of course. He has a very strong case, always assuming that there is nothing objectionable about the poems.

Another Whitemoor prisoner had written to me asking me to call on him. He staggered me a little by saying that his present sentence is forty-two years. He has never committed murder or attempted murder. According to him, the total sentence is due to a string of burglaries. He began stealing quite early and had very little schooling, but he is a practising Catholic and is going to let me know how to make contact with his solicitor.

The sentence of forty-two years apparently boils down to twenty-six years to be served. No doubt at least one escape comes into the story. All the same, I can't help hoping that some reduction can be secured somehow.

Friday May 28, 1999

I spent half an hour with the director of high-security prisons, formerly governor of Whitemoor. I was anxious to find out what possible reason could be produced for refusing to allow Des Nilsen to publish his poems. The only reason the excellent director could provide was that they would be sold for money, even though Des would not receive a penny and it would all go to charity. I am putting down a question accordingly in the House of Lords.

Something that the director said left me with a lurking suspicion that the real reason for banning publication is that there would be an outcry by victims and friends of victims, including no doubt the tabloids. This would be a reason they might not wish to disclose. So we shall see where we get to when the question is asked.

Sunday May 30, 1999

Visited my old friend David Rundle at the house of an old friend in Bognor Regis.

David was sentenced to life for killing his wife in the course of a row. He completed his sentence thirteen years ago, but over five years later he is still technically a prisoner, though he seems to receive a good deal of home leave. It all seems to date from allegations made by a bitter woman after his original release. He still has the same probation officer who reported adversely on him at that time and got him sent back to prison.

This time it does seem that the Parole Board are favourable to his release. I am waiting to hear from him as to whom to approach. He was in excellent form and it was good to see the friendship between him and his host.

Wednesday June 2, 1999

Made the long trek to see Eddie Richardson at Long Lartin in Worcestershire. Of all the prisoners I have known I think of him as 'Mr Might-have-been'. After coming out of prison many years ago he made good in business and managed to secure education for two striking daughters, one of them now a ballet instructor with 130 pupils, the other a university-trained chemist.

But somehow he got entangled with drugs and is now serving twenty-five years for helping to import them.

I had a rather ghastly experience in the course of my

visit. Long Lartin Prison is seven miles from Evesham. I was relying for lunch (drink and sandwich) on the existence of a pub close to the prison. When I got there it was closed. Eventually a kindly prison officer took me into the officers' mess where I got something to eat. But no doubt it was good for me to be forced to go for one day without a drink at lunch.

Tuesday June 8, 1999

Made my way to the Old Bailey for the sentencing of Jonathan Aitken, who had pleaded guilty to perjury. I stayed an hour. The case went on all day and at the end the judge sent him to prison for eighteen months, which was less than his friends had feared.

Monday June 14, 1999

Elizabeth and I set off for the annual lunch and service of the Knights of the Garter. I am, as it happens, after twenty-eight years the senior knight and one of the 'oldsters' who attempted the walk from Windsor Castle to St George's Chapel for the service. As I approached the latter building an urgent message arrived from the Queen to persuade me to enter by a side door, a request with which I felt bound to comply. In fact going up the steps to the chapel would not have troubled me, but I was not the only knight who was haunted by the thought of the steps down. In the event an official sprang forward to give me an arm down.

Antonia has recently joined Elizabeth and her husband Harold as a CBE. She received a warm message of congratulations from Prince Charles. Elizabeth and I were quick to thank him and his mother as they passed us by. He was as charming as ever, but a lonely figure.

Wednesday June 16, 1999

Visited Jonathan Aitken. A hired car provided by the generosity of Harold Pinter took an hour to convey me to Belmarsh Prison near Woolwich. I am glad that my friend John Kay, chief reporter of *The Sun*, published my statement afterwards that it was the most inspiring visit I had paid in fifty years of prison visiting.

Jonathan Aitken, always religious, is now filled with a strong sense of God's presence. He is studying for a theology degree, learning New Testament Greek, and has started a Bible class. He hopes to become an Anglican clergyman in due course.

I had heard that he was reading Thomas à Kempis, and duly turned back to the beginning of *The Imitation of Christ*. I told him that I felt that Thomas's approach to Christ seemed to me almost too remote from his fellow humans. But Jonathan, after twenty-five years in the House of Commons, is at ease with his fellow men and is receiving warmth and kindness from fellow prisoners who have, in some cases, committed the most serious crimes.

Monday June 21, 1999

A rather surprising Question Time in the Lords. I put down a question asking whether the government would reconsider the refusal to allow Des Nilsen to publish his poems, in view of the fact that he would be giving the proceeds to charity.

The week before I had been preparing myself for a negative answer. Then last Friday I received a message from the private secretary to the Home Office minister, Gareth Williams, apologising that his planned reply to me had been leaked to the press, and might well be appearing in *The Independent* the following day. (In fact it did so, though I did not know this until after I had asked my question today.)

The news she brought me was welcome. The minister would, in fact, be allowing Des Nilsen to publish his poems, subject to a number of conditions which were not unreasonable.

Today, therefore, I was preparing to congratulate the minister on an enlightened change of mind, due to his personal intervention. In fact, he gave an answer which I am fairly bound to describe as disingenuous. He did not admit that there had been any change, but simply stated the present ruling as though it had always been in force. This was a bit rich, considering that the minister himself had written to me confirming the ban.

I asked Lord Mason, former Secretary of State for Northern Ireland sitting beside me, whether I had been too rude to my own front bench. He replied, 'Marginal.'

When I finally read *The Independent* article, I rang the journalist who wrote it and discovered that the minister's office had circulated not only my question, but also the proposed answer, last Friday. Friends in the House of Lords are horrified when I tell them this.

Friday July 2, 1999

Visited Jonathan Aitken in Stamford Hill Prison, Isle of Sheppey. The journey from there to Hurst Green was very expensive, though I took a bus from Maidstone.

When I got out of the train at Sittingbourne to take a taxi for the twelve-mile trip to the prison the driver introduced me to a new phrase: 'Money up front' – in other words, cash before we started. He explained that some visitors to prisons defaulted when it came to the point. He said that if I had looked like a barrister, he would not have made the demand. After the visit, when we set off for Maidstone, he did not repeat the request, having discovered by that time that I had been a member of the House of Lords for a long time.

I am very glad that I was able to see Jonathan again, bringing messages particularly from *The Spectator* party which I had attended the evening before. I was afraid that following his transfer to this prison he would rather miss the exhilaration of close association with a number of serious criminals, who took to him instantly. He has had to give up his Bible class just as he was starting, but he was as wise as ever and wants now to settle down to serious reading for his theology degree.

There has been some criticism of his widespread publicity, including his publication of a poem, about which there are various opinions.

Thursday July 8, 1999

A long journey, made possible by the generosity of Harold Pinter, to visit a patient in the low-security ward of the Edgware Hospital. He was not there because of any criminal conviction, but because his schizophrenia had apparently made him a local nuisance. His sister had begged me to visit him because she feared that he was starving himself to death, but the hospital took a fairly relaxed view of this possibility; after a month's nominal hunger strike his weight had only gone down by eleven pounds.

I was particularly glad to visit him for three reasons. One, his only other visitor, his sister, has been banned on the suspicion, unproved, that she was bringing in alcohol. Two, I discovered that there were no educational classes in this hospital whereas in prison such classes would almost certainly have existed. Three, he appeared somewhat inarticulate and was obviously treated as a mental case by the staff.

But before I left he handed me about a dozen poems. He

declaimed the first one of them to us and I think that the psychiatrist and the nurse shared my good opinion of it. I promised to do my best to get one, at least, of his poems printed.

Monday August 2, 1999

Visited a new prisoner, Robert Gleave, at Maidstone. A heatwave led me to make the visit without a coat. I was disconcerted on arrival to be told that I must present proof of identity, which of course I had left behind in my coat pocket. Eventually a charming female duty governor arrived who looked after me for the rest of the afternoon, so my treatment was a mixture of plus and minus.

Gleave is an unusual figure. He has the build of a traditional alderman, and certainly did not look down on his luck, but he is serving a sentence of fifteen years for buggery and attempted buggery which would discourage most people. He had a wife and four children but is now divorced.

He discussed such matters without embarrassment. He is very critical of the failure of Maidstone to provide adequate education services compared, for example, with Brixton where he came from. What adds strength to his argument is the fact that he served in Maidstone twelve or thirteen years ago when the educational services, he claims, were much better.

The duty governor joined us at the end of the interview and seemed quite happy with my readiness to take up the matter with the minister.

Wednesday August 4, 1999

Visited Father Fred for the first time in Dartmoor. Making the arrangements was a nightmare. They insisted that I must have a visiting order which meant getting him to send me one at short notice. (I have, however, taken up the matter with the minister.) It was the first time that I can remember having this trouble. I have long understood that peers and MPs do not require one.

I then had to make my way by taxi the thirty miles from Exeter to the prison. The taxi man only charged me £50 for the return trip, plus an hour's waiting, which was a good deal less than I expected.

Father Fred was his usual self though he cannot pretend to like Dartmoor. The crucial point is that he was transferred to Dartmoor in order to take a sex-offender's course regarded as essential for parole. On arrival he learnt that the course would not start until next summer. I have now written to the new Minister for Prisons, Paul Boateng, to ask for an interview. I shall argue that Grendon Underwood Prison is the only proper destination for Father Fred at this stage.

Friday August 6, 1999

Visited Jonathan Aitken at Stamford Hill Prison. It is a good twelve miles from the station. The journey back to Bernhurst cost me a small fortune last time. This time, however, my ever more valued friend Andrew McCooey met me at Maidstone.

Jonathan is studying for his theological degree with the possibility of becoming a clergyman. He wakes at five every morning and spends the next two hours in prayer and Bible reading. So we all had a good religious confabulation.

Jonathan told us that he has a prayer partner, a Roman Catholic. Although he is an Anglican, Jonathan recently became godfather to his prayer partner's baby. At the end Jonathan delivered a wonderful prayer, and I did my best in my turn.

He certainly has an electric quality similar to Tony Blair.

I am not surprised to hear, as in Belmarsh, he has founded a flourishing prayer group.

We were all amused to hear what happened when he was visited by his friend Michael Howard, author of the famous phrase 'prison works', whom I called the prince of darkness when he was Home Secretary. This time Howard arrived with two Special Branch detectives to guard him against assault from prisoners.

He was (deliberately it seems) kept standing for a long time outside the prison. Eventually he and the two guards and Jonathan sat down together in the visiting room. It appears that the prisoners were nice to him. Not so the officers.

I am a little surprised that he is not a hero with the prison staff. Perhaps, however, the fifty per cent increase in the prison population while he was Home Secretary was the reason.

Interview with Lord Longford About His Prison Visiting

Why do you do it?

I do not suppose that anyone can answer that question about themselves very successfully. I have always had, looking back, what is sometimes described as a 'social conscience', though I am not implying that that necessarily leads one into social work.

My father, a professional soldier, died at the head of his brigade at Gallipoli during the First World War. My brother dedicated himself to Irish theatre. He took his Dublin company all round Ireland. When he died in 1961 there was a minute's silence for him in the Dublin theatres.

I do not suggest that my sense of a duty to my fellow men has been more acute than theirs, but it has been very different. My model, in retrospect, though never consciously adopted, must have been my maternal uncle, Arthur Villiers, a younger son of the Earl of Jersey. He was an extremely successful business man, a partner in Barings Bank when it was the crème de la crème, and a decorated soldier in the First World War.

Apart from the war years he lived the whole of his adult life in Hackney, east London, where he presided over Eton Manor, then the largest boys' club in Britain. I spent many nights at the club over the years, played for them in their first rugby match, and regularly went into camp with them at Cuckoo Weir, Eton.

I hasten to add that for sixty-eight years I have been married to a lady with a social conscience even more acute than mine. It was derived, partly at least, from her father and brother – Harley Street specialists – and her mother, a niece of Joseph Chamberlain.

If not originally, then I have become more and more aware of my privileged circumstances; a title or two may or may not help. I stepped out of the property and lands that were my Irish inheritance when my brother died childless and I succeeded only to the family title. But I was given a first-class education at Eton and Oxford without paying for it, and have inherited a delightful place in Sussex.

Many a sermon at Eton urged us privileged boys to give something back to the society that had been so good to them. Hardly any of my school colleagues ever became Labour in politics, but collectively they have done an enormous amount for various charities.

Why did you choose prisons?

Accident came into it. In 1936 I became a member of the Labour party, having some years before worked for the Conservative Research Department. I was already a Christ Church don and soon afterwards became a city councillor in Oxford.

I boldly announced, 'I am a socialist because I am a Christian.' I was already familiar with the words of Christ, 'I was in prison and you came to see me.' To become a visitor in the Oxford prison followed, it seemed, inevitably.

Do you believe that punishment in prison has any worth?

I have had my say on punishment in countless ways over the years, notably in debates in the House of Lords and in my books, *Punishment and the Punished* (1991), *Prisoner or Patient* (1992) and *Young Offenders* (1993). But the gist of my analysis was conveyed as long ago as 1961 in my small book *The Idea of Punishment*.

I took it for granted, I suppose, as I do now, that an ordered society would be impossible without some kind of punishment for those who broke its rules. I distinguished four traditional elements in a just punishment: deterrence, prevention (keeping law breakers out of mischief), retribution and reform – now usually called rehabilitation. I added reparation, though recognising the extreme difficulty of arranging that in most cases.

I still accept that basic analysis, but the whole thing in my eyes breaks down morally if reform or rehabilitation are left out of the equation. In the years after 1933 there was a grave danger of exactly that, but now the situation appears once more to be changing – in which direction I am still not sure.

How do you judge innocence or guilt among those you visit?
That is not a question I ask myself when I visit a fellow human being in custody. In nearly every case he will have asked for help, or his family will have asked if I could try to help him. But help certainly does not mean trying to help him escape.

It more frequently means trying to get the conditions of his life in prison improved. Sometimes it means trying to get his sentence modified; sometimes, but very infrequently, it means trying to get him liberated at once.

I suppose that I do not make much effort of the last kind unless I feel that there is a plausible case to be made. I very seldom feel quite sure that a prisoner is innocent, and even when I do I seldom win the battle. But, over the years, I have had successes even in this last area.

Myra Hindley is an example of a prisoner who, on any reckoning, including her own, deserved punishment, but nothing comparable to the vindictive persecution she has received and the sentence she has already served for more than thirty years.

But I must bring in here a more controversial proposition. No one who has for many years visited prisoners, some of whom have committed appalling crimes, can easily believe that human beings can be divided into good people and bad people. I leave out the vital fact that the line between those who are mentally ill and those who are judged fully responsible can never be drawn with any confidence.

When I visit, for example, my friend Des Nilsen and recognise to the full my advantages and his disadvantages, I simply do not believe that we human beings at least can make any sense of the statement that I am booked for heaven and he for the other place. After all these years of prison visiting I am more than ever certain that when we pass away, except perhaps for a few saints, we shall all require a long process of purification.

How do you react when prisoners reject you?

There are, I am sure, countless prisoners who have no desire whatever for me to visit them. But, with rare exceptions, I only visit prisoners at their own request, or at the request of their relatives. Two exceptions are Des Nilsen, and the so-called 'Yorkshire Ripper'. In each case I was writing a book and asked to visit them as part of my research. I visited the 'Ripper' just once, but have become a friend of Des Nilsen whom I have been visiting regularly for about eight years.

It is unusual for a prisoner to cease being friendly towards me. I remember, however, one case where a man wanted a sex change to become a woman and was dissatisfied with my efforts on his behalf.

Ian Brady, for many years now in Ashworth Special Hospital, had turned against me – understandably perhaps – because in trying to lessen the guilt of Myra, I inevitably seemed to increase his own. He was reported by the press as describing me as a 'Home Office lackey', a description that department would be unlikely to recognise.

More recently – after a break of ten years – he asked to see me somewhat urgently and we had a friendly talk. At the time of writing fresh controversy seems to be breaking out between him and Myra, so I make no predictions about the future.

When a prisoner comes out we tend to lose contact,

although the decision is not mine. I became very friendly with Christopher Craig who was too young to be hanged when Derek Bentley suffered that fate. I wrote to him recently to say how happy I was about the Bentley pardon.

Sometimes a prisoner maintains a pen-friendship, while not welcoming visits. Myra Hindley is the outstanding example. I began visiting her thirty years ago. In the last few years she has not felt a visit from me would be helpful because of the press interest aroused and the inevitable photographers hanging about outside the prison. Yet she has maintained an affectionate correspondence, referring to me, for example, as her 'Robbie Ross' whom we remember as a friend of Oscar Wilde. When Oscar was led manacled from the court after his conviction, Robbie stood outside and reverently raised his hat.

More recently I am glad to think Myra has welcomed the resumption of visits. Elizabeth and I have had more than one encouraging time with her at High Point Prison in Suffolk. It is good to see the warmth with which she and Elizabeth embrace each other.

How do you react when prison officials and Home Office ministers treat you badly?

I must distinguish here. I personally have never been unreasonably treated by a minister, although their attitude to my representations has often been very unsatisfactory and sometimes has appalled me. When I first became active in making representations on behalf of a prisoner in the early 1950s, I had already been First Lord of the Admiralty and so on, and ministers do not treat such people in a way that makes them seem discourteous.

I have certainly been treated harshly, for want of a better word, in many prison visits, but so have countless others. Prison visitors have a tough time which, on the whole, is getting tougher. I try to put myself in the position of prison officers who are coping with a visiting population which includes many 'baddies'. When they make a perfunctory search of me, I sometimes ask whether they ever discover anything on anybody. They always reply, 'Frequently.' We are all aware that prisons are said to be full of drugs, which presumably slip in through the visitors.

In my diaries I have given some examples of the tiresome treatment of visitors. Whitemoor, perhaps, is somewhat of an extreme case because it was discovered there that guns were slipping in. I accept that taking off one's shoes is not unreasonable. I find it harder to believe that drugs can be concealed in the toe of a walking stick.

What is incontrovertible is that, even in the same prison, the search varies from visit to visit. Only once, it is true, was my belt removed at Whitemoor. Only twice was I made to put out my tongue in case I might be intending to kiss a male inmate and transfer some drugs at the same time. The truth is, however, that within certain limits it is a matter of chance what kind of investigation one would be submitted to.

An extreme example, perhaps, can be provided from another prison. I was actually being escorted by an official and one of his colleagues. He demanded proof of my identity. He was dissatisfied with my bus pass, though it contained a photograph of me. The governor's permission had to be obtained for me to proceed.

Do I get angry? In retrospect, angrier than I would like to think. Afterwards one can see that it is all part of the day's work. One is left brooding on the question of whether it is inevitable in view of the special security dangers in the case of prisons. In practice one is left with a fresh resolution: keep ventilating criticisms to the authorities. Without, I hope, undue arrogance, I say to myself, if I don't protest, no one else will.

Do you mind being mocked by the press on account of your prison visits?

I have never been mocked by the kind of newspapers that my friends admit to reading. The tabloids have derided me for many years and certainly people treat me as someone who has faced much unpopularity.

I suppose that if I had been a member of the Commons I would have paid a heavy price for supporting Myra Hindley. In the Lords, I have never encountered hostility or derision. I am left wondering whether I would have had the guts to persist with my kind of campaign if I had not led this privileged life in the House of Lords.

Since I have turned ninety, the danger is the other way. I have been called saintly in *The Guardian* and the *Evening Standard*. I have two friends in the popular press, John McEntee (editor of the William Hickey column) and John Kay, chief reporter of *The Sun*. The latter has referred to me as one of the most charming people you could meet.

When I visited Jonathan Aitken recently at Stamford Hill Prison, the *Sunday Mirror* devoted almost a page to the photograph of Jonathan, myself and Andrew McCooey, a one-man solicitor's firm recently appointed an assistant judge, to the delight of his many friends. The gospel readers are aware of the dangers that attend us when all men speak well of us.

What do your visits offer a prisoner?

As I said earlier, I nearly always visit prisoners when they or their families have asked me to do so. The fact that in nearly all cases, until they leave prison, prisoners are anxious for me to continue the visits indicates that they feel that they derive some encouragement from them.

I myself have derived enormous benefit from the visits. They have been described by a more or less friendly critic as 'my passport to heaven', but I do not bank on that. I suppose that as a member of the most privileged body in the world, the House of Lords, it is, to say the least, a good corrective.

How effective can you be on a prisoner's behalf?

One would really have to ask a Home Office official, or more than one, as to how much attention in practice is paid to my representations. The one thing that I feel sure about is that more attention is paid to the prisoner as a result of them.

Not long ago a prisoner complained to me after my visit that he was twice stripped and searched and, in spite of physical disability, made to stand without support. When challenged, the prison officer denied it, but the relevant governor took a friendly interest and I should be surprised if it happens again.

Forty years ago I took up the case of Michael Davies, convicted of his share in the so-called 'Clapham Common murders'. I believed him innocent. After endless wrangling he was released after seven years which I suppose in a small way was a victory for him and me.

I took up recently the question of the publication of Des Nilsen's poems which had been refused by the Minister for Prisons on the recommendation, I suppose, of the governor. Permission in principle has since been granted, subject to various conditions. At the time of writing I remain hopeful that they will see the light of day. One of them has already been published on the front page of *Inside Time*, a paper which is written mainly by prisoners.

How do you reconcile your privileged status in the Lords with visiting prisons?

This question shows an innocence of the Upper House. It has never been remotely unpopular to take up the case of individual prisoners. That would be true even in 1957 when the House of Lords rejected the bill passed by the House of Commons on a free vote which would have abolished capital punishment. The former Lord Chief Justice on that occasion expressed the feelings of many when referring to a particular murderer. He said that such a man should be destroyed.

But the bill had been introduced into the Lords by Lord Templewood, a former Conservative Home Secretary, and no one in any party offered any criticism of its supporters, then or later. A former Minister of State (and Leader of the House) Lord Windlesham has written three most important books on penal matters.

What needs to change now?

In the years up to 1993 there was, speaking generally, a slow but steady improvement in the prison situation. Then came Michael Howard, the Home Secretary, fully supported by the Cabinet, with the slogan, 'prison works'. In four years the numbers increased by fifty per cent, although crime was, if anything, declining.

Labour came into power in 1997 with its own slogan, 'Tough on crime, tough on the causes of crime'. After they had been in office a year, it was impossible to point to any improvement in the situation. But since then the prison population has been stabilised, and the Home Secretary – in a notable speech to the Prison Reform Trust in 1998 – pointed a new way forward. There is every reason to think that the 'tagging' of prisoners towards the end of their sentence will reduce the numbers in custody.

Other legislation, however, points in the opposite direction. It is impossible at the moment to make any serious forecast about future numbers in prison and therefore on the level of treatment.

In a debate I opened on July 12, 1999, I quoted the last report of the Chief Inspector of Prisons, in my eyes just about the best-qualified judge of the prison situation. He was distinctly encouraging to the government for the first time, but a later report of his on Wormwood Scrubs was, as I said in my speech, the most damaging report produced for many years. So the jury is still out, but I am still hopeful that a good Christian socialist like the present Home Secretary will, by the end of his time, be able to point to results which are worthy of his ideals.

The most obvious need is more money, but a new mindset among those in power is even more necessary. If I am asked where I can point to any great change that would alter the whole prison scene so that we could at the same time feel that we were more secure and that prisoners were treated in a more Christian fashion, I would reply in one sentence, 'A great Home Secretary would set out to improve the relationship between the Prison Officers' Association on the one hand and the Prison Service, the Home Office and the government on the other hand.'

At the present time the Prison Officers' Association has no real friends, although now and then half-compliments are paid to them by ministers. Yet I have told them again and again that theirs is the most difficult task in the world, and one of the most important. They really must be taken into the confidence of those who rule our prisons. I have suggested in the House of Lords one small step which would lead in the right direction. The Minister for Prisons is to be provided with a new strategy unit. I beg those in authority to allow a representative of the Prison Officers' Association to serve on it. That would be the beginning of wisdom, but what I am talking about is a change in attitude which would take a long time to achieve.

I have a fear that readers of these diaries will find themselves even less friendly to prison officers than in the past. Naturally someone like myself encounters little difficulties which are very annoying, but no one should ever forget that day in, day out, prison officers perform their onerous duties in a way that would be beyond the competence of most of us.

Has your mission to prisoners been a success?
Others must be left to answer this one. Worldly success is such an ambiguous and relative term. Herbert Morrison and R.A. Butler, for example, are sometimes referred to as failures because they did not become prime ministers. Yet by most standards they were more successful than ninety-nine out of a hundred of us.

If I were to sum up my own achievement I could certainly claim to have befriended many friendless people. Perhaps that is a sufficient claim in itself.

But what can I point to as my legacy? I founded the New Bridge for ex-prisoners and the New Horizon youth centre for young homeless. Both flourish today. No one can take away that source of satisfaction.

I started the first debate on prisons in the House of Lords in 1955 and I have initiated and taken part in many similar debates since that time. It would be very unwise for an individual to claim any personal credit for the improvement that took place for nearly forty years subsequently.

Equally, no penal reformer who has kept pegging away feels guilty because his ideals were denied so abruptly a few years ago. Prisons will always be very imperfect places and sentencing a very imperfect process. I am not claiming that the most successful reformers have necessarily been Christians. Archbishop Temple assuredly was. Barbara Wootton (Baroness Wootton) most assuredly was not. I shall never forget the difficulty they had in finding an alternative form of words for her when I was helping to sponsor her introduction to the Lords, but as far as I am concerned the inspiration has continued to be Christian and takes us wider than prisons. Jesus Christ said, 'I have come to seek and save those who are lost.' To say that I have been successful in living up to that message would be ridiculous and almost blasphemous. But as long as I live I shall continue to try to live up to his words.

Articles

The Tablet, March 1, 1997

The Inside Story

Derek Lewis's book, *Hidden Agendas* (Hamish Hamilton, 1997), will be essential reading for penal students for years to come. It will be a supplement to Lord Windlesham's three volumes, *Responses to Crime*. The last one is a devastating analysis of Michael Howard's record as Home Secretary, based on Lord Windlesham's experience as Minister of State at the Home Office and chairman of the Parole Board (he was also Leader of the House of Lords).

Derek Lewis has had more experience at what might be called the sharp end. He was director-general of the Prison Service for three years until sacked abruptly by the Home Secretary. A born writer, he describes dramatically his dismissal and his subsequent meeting with the Minister for Prisons, Ann Widdecombe, who dissolved in tears.

Perhaps the most telling passage in a compelling book is one where he describes the events leading to his dismissal. The final report by General Learmont arrived on 27 September.

> It was little better than the draft we had seen in May. A few gross inaccuracies had been removed, but no attempt had been made to provide a solid evidential base, or any degree of balance.
>
> The Home Secretary's first thoughts were clearly for himself. Was there anything in it that might require him to resign? The general's covering letter pointed out that criticisms contained

> in the report affected people in the Prison Service through to board level, but that criticism stopped there. This was hardly the case, since the report heavily criticised the ways in which ministers see the service's conflicting objectives.

If one had been Mr Howard, one would have heaved a great sigh of relief. An escape route was offered which could be accepted without obvious dishonour and in the House of Commons he proved fully equal to the task of exonerating himself. If one had been a saint one might have refrained from looking for a scapegoat, but being human he picked on Derek Lewis for the role. In the House of Lords I have described the dismissal of Lewis as contemptible, but who am I to say that in Mr Howard's situation I would have adopted a nobler course?

When Derek Lewis was appointed director-general (by Kenneth Clarke, Michael Howard's predecessor), I said, and repeat, that it was a regrettable appointment because discouraging to the hard-pressed Prison Service. It was bound to give the impression that they could not find a suitable appointee among their own ranks. Since then they have found one, but only because the government could not find someone else from outside to take the job.

Nevertheless, I have come to admire Derek Lewis as a sincere and very able man. I have found as I have gone round the prisons that many officers previously hostile to him had come round to that point of view.

But that does not mean that all wisdom was delivered to him when he became director-general. When he was dismissed, he still had a lot to learn. His remarks in this book about the Prison Officers' Association are unfortunate. If he had spent still more time in prisons, he would realise that theirs is perhaps the most difficult vocation in the world. I remember shouting to a prison officer through a thick glass at Whitemoor, 'You and I would have a better relationship if we didn't have to bawl at each other through this awful thing.' He shouted back, 'You have never had a knife pointed at your throat.'

Derek Lewis is a sensitive man and he would have learned that lesson if he had been given a little longer.

But the issues go wider than the personal clash between Mr Howard and Mr Lewis. The problems of a minister in relation to one of the so-called 'agencies' – in this case the Prison Service – won't go away in a hurry. There will be no easy answers. The minister is held responsible in Parliament for every jot and tittle of what goes on in prison, whether those dealing with prisoners are part of a so-called prison commission, as used to be the case, or ordinary civil servants, as they subsequently became, or members of an 'agency' as they are now. A minister will never be absolved from responsibility for what goes wrong in the prison, including gross breaches of security.

What is clearly essential is that there should be a good working relationship between the minister and the head of the agency, if we must have an agency. Here one must be fair to Michael Howard, not that I often find it easy. Mr Lewis was appointed by Mr Clarke, who, like his predecessors, was broadly concerned with improving life for prisoners. Mr Howard came in with a totally different message – that prison worked and would work better if made more unpleasant for the prisoners. One must make allowances therefore for Mr Howard if he felt that Mr Lewis was not a man after his own heart.

Reading the story as it is told here – and I accept that it is broadly true – it is clear that an opinion was held throughout the Prison Service that Michael Howard was too much actuated by political ambitions. Derek Lewis has tried to be fair to him but in the circumstances has presented a very unflattering portrait. I myself have said recently on television, in regard to Mr Howard's treatment of Myra Hindley, that we must all hope to be forgiven – including Michael Howard.

Frank Longford

The Sun, October 30, 1997

Should Myra Hindley Ever Be Freed?

'YES,' SAYS LORD LONGFORD,
VETERAN CAMPAIGNER FOR MYRA'S RELEASE

Myra Hindley as a very young woman became an infatuated accomplice in crimes of appalling horror. She has been in prison for thirty-one years now. No one outside a loony bin supposes that she would be a danger to anyone if she was released.

Yet despite this, she finds herself endlessly persecuted in the most contemptible fashion.

Myra was a good Roman Catholic girl until the age of eighteen when she began to work under Ian Brady, a mentally afflicted man who has for many years been in a secure mental hospital. She has said she became evil and is more to blame than him because she had not got the excuse of mental disturbance.

She will always be haunted by the horrific crimes in which she was so deeply involved. It would be an understatement to say she feels heartbroken remorse in front of God and the parents of the victims.

Although I have been visiting prisoners for sixty years now I have not forgotten the victims.

I have been asked incessantly over the years, 'What have you done for the victims?' I can only reply, 'Much less than I should like to have done.' But I cannot think of many men in public life who have done more for them.

I opened the first debate on victims in the House of Lords. I introduced the first bill in their favour. I am president of the Matthew Trust which is primarily concerned with mental offenders, but also with victims.

There are two issues about Myra Hindley that must be disentangled. Firstly, how should somebody who has been found guilty of complicity in appalling crimes be treated?

Secondly, how should Hindley be treated after thirty-one years in prison?

The public should be reminded that her original tariff was thirty years. That is the seriousness that was attached to the crime at the time. No one seriously suggests that her crime has got worse over the years.

Whatever treatment should have been meted out to her originally, it would be a gross breach of faith to a fellow human being if new and harsher criteria were suddenly applied.

There is, however, the wider question of whether public attitudes to serious crime could be affected by what they regard as over-lenient treatment.

Whatever view is taken, no humane person can fail to set a limit to the amount of cruelty inflicted on a fellow human being.

We have abolished capital punishment in Britain. And I hope that we shall never go halfway back to it by condemning a deeply repentant sinner to rot and die in prison.

The Times, April 13, 1998

Letters to the Editor

STRAW'S 'ROBUST' CRIME BILL UNDER FIRE

Sir, The Home Secretary's article 'Crime and Old Labour's Punishment' (April 8), contains, as one would expect from an intelligent and high-minded man, many points of substance. I am not concerned here to argue the detailed merits of the Crime and Disorder Bill; insofar as it makes prosecution easier it could be helpful to society. But the heading of the article will horrify anyone with serious concerns for justice in the penal field.

I was chairman in 1964 of a committee set up by Harold Wilson, then Leader of the Opposition, to draw up a plan of penal policy. It contained six members of the subsequent government, whose penal record was equal to anything in our history. It included the abolition of capital punishment and the introduction of parole.

It is simply no use Mr Straw pretending that he has arrived at a new penal policy as a result of personal enlightenment. He is of course aware that the present government has continued the revolutionary approach of Michael Howard, 'prison works'. As a result the Home Office has reckoned that the numbers in prison will have doubled between 1993 and 2005, in spite of no official expectation of an increase in crime.

In recent Lords' debates no one not officially instructed has said a word in favour of Mr Straw's policy. The judiciary and the churches are equally opposed to it.

I am an obsequious follower of the present government, but I can only hope that a good Christian like Mr Straw will have gained new wisdom from his Easter observances.

Yours faithfully,
Frank Longford, House of Lords

The Catholic Herald, August 21, 1998

An Icon of Evil That Belongs in the Past

AN ARTICLE WRITTEN BY LORD LONGFORD
AFTER HIS VISIT TO MYRA HINDLEY

I was sitting in the lobby of the House of Lords when a guide passed by conducting a number of middle-aged ladies from the Midlands. He pointed me out in a friendly fashion as a long-serving member. 'There', he said, 'is Lord Longford. The friend of Myra Hindley.'

I rose to my feet and thanked him for the introduction but pointed out that I had also been Leader of the House of Lords and done one or two other things in my lifetime. Nevertheless I would be happy to be remembered in the way suggested. Taxi drivers sometimes begin by asking me, 'How's Myra?' once again in friendly fashion, in these latter days.

Opinion, not surprisingly, has changed somewhat over the thirty-two years Myra has been in prison. A former Home Office minister went out of his way lately to say that he agreed with me. So did the then editor of a national newspaper. But still *The Sun* is not alone among the tabloids in maintaining a public image of her as an evil monster. The struggle for justice in her case goes on.

I first met Myra Hindley thirty years ago when she had been in prison for about two years. She had written to ask me whether I could help her to meet Ian Brady, the senior partner in the terrible Moors murders. The Home Office, I am glad to think, refused the application and, after a few years, the correspondence between them ceased.

She had been a good Catholic girl before she met him and, after the tragic infatuation which led her to be his accomplice, she had returned to the church, sufficient, it appeared, for the breakdown of the relationship.

She has since expressed overwhelming agonised remorse in a number of ways, public and private. She has described her own part as 'morally worse than his', because she should have been more aware of the evil they were involved in – that she helped to abduct the children with Brady; something he would find difficult to do alone. I got to know Ian Brady quite well first, when he was in prison, and when he was transferred to Ashworth Special Hospital. After a lapse of ten years when he did not want to see me, he asked me to visit him again the other day. It was Myra's unimaginable destiny to come to work under this brilliant, but mentally disturbed young man, with such tragic consequences for the victims and relatives. Many years ago I quoted some letters of his in a book I published. Professor A.L. Rowse wrote to me after reading them: 'He must be a remarkable man.' Painfully true. When I saw him the other day he told me that he was a working-class boy without a known father, and at the age of fifteen had begun reading Dostoevsky. But by the time he met Myra he had already become involved in youthful crime and served a sentence in Borstal. So much for the distant past.

What kind of person is Myra Hindley? I will quote only two opinions. The first woman governor she served under said to me of her, 'Myra is no criminal.' Not long ago the priest who dealt with her closely for four years paid this tribute to her:

> I know that the quiet woman whom I meet twice weekly, who makes me a cup of tea and discusses matters of faith more intelligently and knowledgeably than most church leaders I know, bears absolutely no resemblance to the monstrous image portrayed by the media via a touched-up photograph taken almost thirty years ago.

After the findings of the Divisional Court Tribunal headed by the Lord Chief Justice, the Tribunal decided that Michael Howard, when Home Secretary, had acted unlawfully by not leaving a loophole. The present Home Secretary was held to have left one. But it must remain doubtful whether a Home Secretary will brace himself unaided to do the right and Christian thing by reopening her chance of freedom.

At the time of writing I pin my hopes on the higher judiciary and although now ninety-two I look forward to welcoming her when at last justice is done.

What of her future? It is a long time since I have met anybody who would produce a reputable argument to my face for keeping her in prison. It should be mentioned here that the Parole Board has recommended that she should go to an open prison, usually regarded as a step on the way to release. It is sometimes said, 'Surely you can't imagine any Home Secretary daring to release her in view of the unpopularity that he would incur?'

Caiaphas would have sympathised with that view. It is expedient, he said, that one man should die for the people. But I would hope that Caiaphas has no admirers nowadays. No one can possibly argue that she is dangerous. Her record in prison after an early attempt at escape has been impeccable, including the obtaining of an Honours Degree in the Open University.

Yet she has been told officially that in her case 'life means life'. The only excuse for such a piece of cruelty must be the view taken of the horrific character of the crimes. But this argument crumples when it is pointed out that the first tariff set her was twenty-five years by the Lord Chief Justice; later it became thirty years set by the Home Secretary of the day. It cannot seriously be contended that, as the years have passed, her crimes have got worse.

The Catholic Herald, May 28, 1999

The Haunting Fear of Being Soft on Crime

CHARTERHOUSE CHRONICLE

Jack Straw as Home Secretary has to take controversial decisions every day of the week. Usually I approve these days. To take a small example, I sympathise with his desire to limit the publicity of prostitutes. Exceptionally he does something which is indefensible. He has continued the policy introduced by his predecessors of deciding that certain prisoners should stay in prison for life. Admittedly he has left a loophole for exceptional progress. Myra Hindley, thirty-three years in prison, a good religious woman, has had her so-called tariff increased to this point though no one supposes that the terrible crimes could have got worse.

I hope and pray that the law courts will decide otherwise. But that is one blot on what is beginning to emerge as the message of this good Christian socialist. It is not difficult to understand his fundamental dilemma. A little while before the election a member of the front bench in the House of Lords said to me exultantly, 'We've neutralised the Tories on law and order.' Labour won many votes in the general election on the slogan 'tough on crime, tough on the causes of crime'. Any Labour Home Secretary would be haunted by the fear of being called soft on crime.

For the first year of the present government, it was impossible to distinguish their penal policy from that of Michael Howard, who coined the immortal phrase, 'prison works'. It will be recalled that in the four years of Michael Howard's reign the prison population increased by fifty per cent although there was no increase in crime. That process continued during the first year of the present government but in the last year there has been something of a decline.

This government, like other governments, disclaims responsibility for the sentencing atmosphere, but if one is going to say that Howardism increased the prison population so dramatically, one must allow credit to this government and to Jack Straw in particular for the present decline. In addition there has been a very substantial allocation of new resources, which becomes all the more significant if in fact the prison population stays where it is or even drops.

Replying to a debate I initiated in January, Lord Williams of Mostyn, Minister for Prisons and a very successful performer in the House, struck a triumphant note. 'It is', he declared, 'almost impossible for me to describe the transformation in attitude towards dealing with crime, its prevention, its deterrence and public protection, that has occurred since May of last year.' At the end of his speech I could not help commenting that as a regular visitor to prisons I couldn't yet see any difference on the ground. He, not surprisingly, retorted that his experience was different from mine.

Now, in May, I would be more charitable, though beneficent results cannot be expected to flow at once from an improvement in the attitude of the government. For the first time, this week a prisoner whom I have been visiting regularly asked to be excused on this occasion because he was attending an educational class every day of the week. A small sign but a good one.

The time for canonisation is not yet, however. A Tory proposal has been confirmed which will come into operation next year and which will increase the prison population by several thousand. But for the moment Jack Straw is beginning to rank among penal reform Home Secretaries, which I would not have dared to predict a year ago.

If there is one man whose opinion I would value on this

precise subject, it is the Chief Inspector of Prisons, General Sir David Ramsbotham. In his last annual report, published in February, he told us that the report was written in a very different climate from that in which he was reporting last year: 'My optimism, and gut feeling, that the Prison Service has been presented with another window of opportunity is, this time, not based on a particular disaster, but on a situation that has been created by the very deliberate programme embarked upon by the government in general and the Home Secretary in particular, which I hope I have interpreted correctly.'

In a lecture to the New Bridge organisation for ex-prisoners on May 19 he spoke enthusiastically about steps being taken to bring together the main government departments and voluntary organisations involved in this area.

When the history of this time has to be written I'm sure that the report of the Home Affairs' Committee of the House of Commons published last July will be treated as highly significant. They demanded a substantial reduction in the prison population. The chairman, Chris Mullen, achieved historic triumphs many years ago in the release of the Birmingham Six and Guildford Four. So the signs of penal improvement are favourable but reformers must redouble rather than relax their efforts.

Visiting prisons every week, I always learn something new, possibly more than one thing. A taxi driver taking me from the station to a well-known prison last week had been a prison officer for many years until he recently retired. He had thoroughly enjoyed his time in the service but he described it happily as a life of hazards. He had only been twice assaulted physically, once having his nose broken. But even in my rugger-playing days I would not have liked to tackle him. Others of slighter build might be less fortunate. And what of the women who have introduced a gentler form of treatment?

In that high-security prison they stamp your wrist to

make sure that the person whose pass enables him or her to go in is the same person who comes out. The officer on this occasion asked to see my visiting order. Maybe too grandly, I replied, 'I am a member of the House of Lords. I don't need a visiting order.' He, perhaps understandably miffed, told me, 'I'm not going to have you teaching me my job.' The discussion then became heated. But bearing in mind my responsibility to *The Catholic Herald*, I finished by making a humble apology. I need hardly say that when I left the prison – which I visit often – they didn't even bother to look at my wrist. But I learned my lesson. Don't try to be clever at the expense of those who control your immediate destiny. Prison officers have one of the hardest tasks in the world. Neither I nor most of my friends could do it. I respect and honour them.

Frank Longford

The Catholic Herald, August 6, 1999

Dispensing Rough Justice to the Possibly Dangerous

Mental offenders are back in the news and likely to stay there off and on for many a day. The government has brought forward proposals which, after full discussion, are intended to place in custody a small number of persons allegedly dangerous who have not been convicted by the courts or judged to be mentally sick.

They summarise their plans in this way:

(1) The right balance is struck between the interests of individuals and of society;

(2) The package meets the needs of this group of people better than the present patchy provision;

(3) It is firmly grounded in evidence from research, and capable of adapting over time as new research evidence comes forward;

(4) It provides better value for money than the present arrangements;

(5) It leads in time to a reduction in the level of the most serious offending by people with severe personality disorders, as better preventive measures are identified and implemented, and through the early identification and detention of those who are dangerous.

A howl of protest has, not surprisingly, gone up from those whose lives are dedicated to human rights. They ask where it will stop. It is a method traditionally employed by dictators for incarcerating their opponents. I understand their strength of feeling but I find myself in sympathy with the late Edward VIII who, on the famous occasion said, 'something must be done'. It appears that 2,000 people will initially come under consideration, all suffering from dangerous personality disorders. But of those only 200 are not already in custody.

There have been recent cases in England which have created public support for the government initiative. A recent American tragedy focuses our thoughts. A Mr Barton was suspected some years ago of murdering his first wife. There was not enough evidence to prosecute him. Now he has murdered his second wife, two children and about a dozen businessmen. He left a note saying that he dearly loved his wife and children but regarded the businessmen as responsible for his financial failure. The first reaction is to say, 'clearly bonkers'. The second, 'Why on earth was he not put inside prison or hospital long ago?' Whether or not he would be dealt with in that way under the government's new proposals if he had lived in the UK is not clear. But at least his case helps us concentrate on the problem.

I have been close to the issues involved for many years. When I first became a prison visitor in Oxford in the late 1930s I paid regular visits to a young arsonist, sometimes in prison, sometimes in Littlemore Hospital. It seemed to depend on the whim of the authorities which way he was regarded. In 1940 a close Oxford friend of Elizabeth and myself was sent to Broadmoor. Her husband had died tragically. She went off her head, killed one of her children and tried to kill herself. I visited her in Broadmoor where she made a good recovery. She married a fellow inmate and when they left Broadmoor they lived happily ever after.

Nearly twenty years later a gifted young public relations officer called Peter Thompson called on me and persuaded me to lead a powerful committee investigating the aftercare of prisoners. Its report had far-reaching consequences for prison aftercare. Not long afterwards he suffered a sudden breakdown, attacked some au pair girls who got into his car and spent four years in Broadmoor. There was some doubt, I believe, among the medical staff about the risks involved in his release (a relevant topic today), but since then he has founded the Matthew Trust which has done enormous work for mental offenders. I am honoured to be its president today.

In 1992 I published my book *Prisoner or Patient* dealing with the eternal problem of when someone who commits a crime is to be punished and when he is to be treated as a sick person. Already by that time three men convicted of killing had begun a sentence in prison and were by that time in secure hospitals. Ian Brady (whom I have visited many times); Ronald Kray now dead (several times) and Peter Sutcliffe, the Yorkshire Ripper (once in Broadmoor). I wrote also about Des Nilsen whom I have visited many times in prison and have come to regard as a friend. His crimes are so unbelievable that at first sight one would have assumed that he was a mental case, but he has never been regarded as such and has always insisted on taking full regretful responsibility.

What does all this personal experience lead me towards? The first conclusion is not very helpful: whatever justice is attempted in these borderline cases will be rough justice. Coming to the government's proposals it is easy to say that no one can assess the risks of such persons offending again with any accuracy. But assessment of justice is, to some extent at least, already implicit in the ordinary sentencing process. When I wrote a small book in 1961 called *The Idea of Punishment* I distinguished four elements in a just punishment: retribution, deterrence, reform and prevention. As soon as one mentions prevention one is asking judges to assess the possibility of the offender doing the same again. The assessment of risks is more obvious among life prisoners. They do not obtain parole until it is assumed that it is safe to let them out. Here again human judgment is very fallible. I am in touch with one prisoner, an old friend by now, who has had splendid reports from the prison but has recently been denied removal from category A status on grounds that amount to nothing except perhaps a vague suspicion that he has criminal associates outside. Nevertheless, human judgment is all we've got. I am open to conviction about the possibility of making reasonable assumptions about the 200 prisoners mentioned earlier who are now at liberty and under government plans might find themselves in custody. But I shall look long and hard at the plans for setting up this kind of tribunal that can perform the prodigious feat of combining reasonable security for the public and fair play for the human beings involved.

Frank Longford

Epilogue

Justice for Myra

Just as this book was going to press, the House of Lords – or rather five Law Lords sitting under that title – announced that they had rejected Myra Hindley's request to set aside the Home Office ruling that in her case a life sentence should mean literally life. This Home Office ruling, if unchanged, will result in her dying behind bars.

Though disappointing, the Law Lords' decision is not the last word and in effect leaves us exactly where we were. Myra's legal team still have two routes open to them. The most obvious is an appeal to the European Court of Justice, where a similar Home Office ruling to extend the term of imprisonment of the two youngsters who killed James Bulger was deemed unlawful. It will be remembered that, after the trial judge deemed her capable of reform, she was originally allocated a tariff – or anticipated length of sentence – of thirty years, but this was changed by recent Home Secretaries.

The other route relies on the acceptance by the Law Lords that it would be possible for the Home Secretary to release Myra on proof of her exceptional progress. The Law Lords specifically called upon the Home Secretary to keep the 'life means life' ruling under review in her case. No one who knows anything at all about Myra doubts that she has indeed already made exceptional progress in the thirty-five years she has been in prison. It is hard to think what further progress she could be expected to make. I have known her for thirty of those thirty-five and can vouch for what she has achieved already, as can the string of priests who have visited her and believe her faith to be sincere and well-founded.

So the struggle continues and her friends remain hopeful, but realistic. The judgment of the Law Lords is, of course, strictly legalistic, confining itself to the question of whether the attitude towards her of the Home Secretary is lawful. They did not attempt to cope with the question of whether it is unjust.

I have said more than once since the judgment was announced that keeping Myra in prison like this is taking us halfway back to capital punishment. The attitude of successive Home Secretaries has been to look at her in terms of what she did all those years ago and to pay no heed to her efforts since she has been in prison. I consider that quite unchristian, whether it be applied to Myra or any other prisoner.

It is beyond doubt that this particular attitude has its roots in what is called public opinion. *The Sun* newspaper continues to call Myra a monster and tell its readers that she is a monster. Home Secretaries take notice of that. It is a terrible reflection on Britain today that this horrifying persecution continues. If the facts about her today were made available, I feel confident that people, public opinion if you like, would at heart prefer to see Myra treated with justice.

Index of Names